THE EURO

THE EURO

A Concise Introduction to European Monetary Integration

Madeleine O. Hosli

LYNNE
RIENNER
PUBLISHERS

BOULDER
LONDON

Published in the United States of America in 2005 by
Lynne Rienner Publishers, Inc.
1800 30th Street, Boulder, Colorado 80301
www.rienner.com

and in the United Kingdom by
Lynne Rienner Publishers, Inc.
3 Henrietta Street, Covent Garden, London WC2E 8LU

Library of Congress Cataloging-in-Publication Data
Hösli, Madeleine.
    The euro : a concise introduction to European monetary integration /
        Madeleine O. Hosli.
    Includes bibliographical references and index.
    ISBN 1-58826-376-2 (hardcover: alk. paper)
    ISBN 1-58826-352-5 (pbk.: alk. paper)
    1. Monetary unions—European Union countries. 2. Monetary policy—
European Union countries. 3. European Union countries—Economic integration.
4. Euro. 5. Economic and Monetary Union. 6. European Monetary System
(Organization) I. Title.
HG925.H67 2005
332.4'94—dc22

                                                                2005011007

British Cataloguing in Publication Data
A Cataloguing in Publication record for this book
is available from the British Library.

Printed and bound in the United States of America

        The paper used in this publication meets the requirements
 ∞ of the American National Standard for Permanence of
        Paper for Printed Library Materials Z39.48-1992.

    5 4 3 2 1

Contents

Tables and Figures

Tables

Acknowledgments

This book has benefited from comments and suggestions by many people over time. A much earlier version of Chapter 6 appeared in a previous volume edited by Carolyn Rhodes, *The European Union in the World Community* (Lynne Rienner Publishers). Manuscripts for that volume were discussed at a workshop in Jackson Hole, Wyoming, and I would like to thank participants in that meeting, notably Carolyn Rhodes and Alberta Sbragia, for helpful comments on the draft chapter. Material contained in Chapters 2 and 3 of this book was presented at various scholarly meetings, and helpful feedback by Peter Lange and Jonathan Strand is especially acknowledged in this context. For comments on the entire draft manuscript, I would like to specifically thank Amy Verdun and Peter Loedel. Moreover, the advice provided by Lynne Rienner in the planning and actual writing of this book is highly appreciated.

Various students in graduate seminars at Leiden University in 2003 and 2004 read parts of the manuscript as it developed. I would especially like to thank Nazli Aziz, Pieter Bakker, Anna C. H. Little, and Suying Lai for helpful feedback. Finally, a stimulating environment for the writing of the book was made possible by my husband, Reinoud F. Wolffenbuttel, and by all the happiness and fun we derive from our lively children, whose priorities, fortunately, often differ from those of their parents (because of a focus on salient issues including skating, soccer, bicycling, and hot dogs). Writing this book, in this sense, was an enjoyable (although lengthier than expected) endeavor. I hope reading it will be an equally pleasant experience.

1

Introduction

On January 1, 1999, the euro was created. Eleven European Union (EU) member states located in Western Europe (Austria, Belgium, Finland, France, Germany, Ireland, Italy, Luxembourg, the Netherlands, Portugal, and Spain) entered the European Economic and Monetary Union (EMU). In January 2001, Greece was admitted into the euro area. Former domestic currencies, such as the German mark, the French franc, and the Italian lira, were taken out of circulation in mid-2002.

Why was EMU established, and why was the euro created? This book contends that both economic and political forces drove the incremental process leading to full European monetary unification. Developments both within and outside Europe created pressures, and increased demands, for the gradual establishment of a unified monetary policy and a single currency in Europe. Among the political factors was a perception shared by a range of leading political actors, including government officials and high-level representatives of European institutions (notably the European Commission), that monetary union and the euro would bolster economic gains and deepen the general process of European integration. Core decisionmakers believed economic advantages could be achieved by monetary union and by establishing shields to protect European states from international currency volatility. These perceptions contributed to initiatives launched by major EU state governments, including Germany and France, to establish sound schemes for European monetary cooperation. Predominantly political motives also encouraged efforts to establish patterns of political and economic interdependence that would embed all EU states, including reunified Germany, in a highly institutionalized European framework of monetary and economic governance.

The economic reasons for integration include the aim of economic and political actors to achieve price stability, avoid currency volatility in Europe, and realize a range of transaction cost savings. In addition, increased international economic and financial interdependence, and global trade and capital flows, increasingly created a need for further economic integration. Pressures originating from the general process of economic globalization strengthened incentives for actors within Europe, including major business organizations and interest groups, to deepen monetary cooperation in Europe, with the general aim of increasing Europe's competitiveness in global markets. In this sense, EMU, developed and implemented in a top-down approach, was to constitute the crowning event of a process of gradual economic integration that had led, beginning with early European integration in the late 1950s, to the establishment of Europe's internal market in the beginning of the 1990s.

Generally, the share of EU states in global economic and trade relations appeared to somewhat contradict Europe's low weight in global political affairs. EMU was seen, in the long term, as a tool that might contribute to gradual political integration in Europe by feeding back into the perceptions and identities of a variety of European actors, gradually contributing, in the medium-term future, to the creation of full-fledged political union in Europe.

Hence, the establishment of EMU and its single currency, the euro, can be seen as the result of the interplay of political and economic forces. EMU has been conditioned by developments both endogenous and exogenous to Europe, making EMU and its single currency a fascinating topic to study, especially from an international political economy perspective.

The steps on the road to the creation of full monetary union in Europe have involved establishing regional exchange-rate regimes and a range of steadily deepening institutional structures for European monetary cooperation. These very arrangements, in turn, have influenced perceptions about the feasibility and desirability of EMU. Rationales and motivations of a predominantly economic nature were underlying this steady, although sometimes partially interrupted, process toward full European monetary union. But it clearly took political momentum to realize the implementation of concrete steps, and the institutionalization, of monetary union.

EMU and the euro are now a reality.[1] In spite of the euro's record so far, it is impossible to predict with certainty what the role of this still rather new common currency will be in future global financial and monetary affairs.[2] The European Central Bank (ECB), created in 1998, is still largely in the process of establishing its role and reputation both within Europe and in the global political and monetary context. But its achievements so far, as seen in price stability in Europe and the apparent confidence of global actors in the potential stability of Europe's new currency, are convincing.

EMU is an impressive new enterprise: several advanced industrialized democracies have more or less voluntarily abandoned sovereign policy rights in the domain of monetary politics with the primary aim of achieving collective gains. Current EMU member states will soon be joined by several Central and Eastern Europe states in particular, some of them with fairly promising outlooks regarding economic growth and fiscal balances (as Chapter 5 of this book illustrates). Figure 1.1 shows a map of current EU states participating in the euro area.

Some states in the euro area (notably Germany) were already known for their stable and strong currencies, whereas others were faced with rather frequent decreases in the external value of their domestic units of account. Current members of the euro area have been part of various schemes of European regional monetary cooperation, notably the European Monetary System (EMS) that existed from 1979 until the start of EMU in 1999. The new EU states take part in a follow-up regional monetary scheme, the EMS II.

All EMU member states are part of the EU, with its unique institutional structure, its internal market (a market without internal frontiers), and a membership that seems to be continuously expanding. Not all EU states, however, are members of EMU. Table 1.1 shows which EU states are currently in the euro area, and Table 1.2 provides an overview of EC and EU enlargements in the past. Clearly, many more current EU states will join Europe's monetary union in the future.

As of mid-2005, twelve EU states are members of EMU and thirteen are still nonmembers. Most of the new EU states that joined in 2004, however, can be expected to join the EMU project in the relatively near future. The creation of EMU and the establishment of the euro have certainly affected international economic and financial affairs. Conversely, international monetary relations, patterns of globalization, regionalism, and international competitive pressures may have significantly influenced monetary integration in Europe. In view of these trends, the main aim of this book is to explain what the euro is, how it has come about, and what potential international role it may play in the future. Thus, the main focus of the book is on providing an overview of the history and the possible future of the euro, while illustrating links between political

Figure 1.1 Map of the Euro Area

4

Table 1.1 A List of EU and EMU Member States (2005)

EU member states
Austria*
Belgium*
Cyprus
Czech Republic
Denmark
Estonia
Finland*
France*
Germany*
Greece*
Hungary
Ireland*
Italy*
Latvia
Lithuania
Luxembourg*
Malta
Netherlands*
Poland
Portugal*
Slovak Republic
Slovenia
Spain*
Sweden
United Kingdom

Note: * indicates member of EMU.

and economic forces contributing to the establishment of EMU and its new single currency.

After rather pronounced skepticism, mainly in Europe and in the United States, about whether the euro might ever come into existence, the emphasis in current discussions about EMU appears to have shifted to other topics.[3] It is now simply a fact that the creation of EMU was a realistic endeavor because monetary union has been established. This does not imply, however, that the creation of EMU was considered to be a prudent step by everyone. In fact, some academics saw its establishment as inadequate and premature. However, debate over EMU has now shifted, for the most part, to the question of what the effects of monetary union and the introduction of the euro might be on economic and monetary performance in Europe and in other parts of the world. Will the euro be stable? Will EMU be able to survive potential adverse economic

Table 1.2 Enlargements of the EC and the EU

Member states	EC-6 1958–72	EC-9 1973–80	EC-10 1981–85	EC-12 1986–94	EU-15 1995–2004	EU-25 Since 2004
Austria	–	–	–	–	x	x
Belgium	x	x	x	x	x	x
Bulgaria	–	–	–	–	–	–
Cyprus	–	–	–	–	–	x
Czech Republic	–	–	–	–	–	x
Denmark	–	x	x	x	x	x
Estonia	–	–	–	–	–	x
Finland	–	–	–	–	x	x
France	x	x	x	x	x	x
Germany	x	x	x	x	x	x
Greece	–	–	x	x	x	x
Hungary	–	–	–	–	–	x
Ireland	–	x	x	x	x	x
Italy	x	x	x	x	x	x
Latvia	–	–	–	–	–	x
Lithuania	–	–	–	–	–	x
Luxembourg	x	x	x	x	x	x
Malta	–	–	–	–	–	x
Netherlands	x	x	x	x	x	x
Poland	–	–	–	–	–	x
Portugal	–	–	–	x	x	x
Romania	–	–	–	–	–	–
Slovak Republic	–	–	–	–	–	x
Slovenia	–	–	–	–	–	x
Spain	–	–	–	x	x	x
Sweden	–	–	–	–	x	x
United Kingdom	–	x	x	x	x	x

circumstances (or economic shocks) without too much economic or political upheaval within Europe? Will EMU be beneficial for the EU and for Europe? How about the benign or adverse effects it generates for global actors and on international monetary affairs? Will the euro ever rival the US dollar? These are some of the prominent questions central to discussions about the current and possible future role and significance of the euro.

This book contends that EMU still faces some major challenges, including tensions between the ECB's clear-cut price-stability mandate and preferences of various political actors for a more growth-oriented ECB policy. In addition, when EMU is compared to several federal political systems, the responsibilities for macroeconomic and monetary policy making within EMU appear to be lopsided, with macroeconomic policy making still resting mainly in the hands of national EU governments, in spite of increased attempts at EU-wide coordination and full unification of monetary policy. This asymmetry in policy competencies is partially explained by the fact that not all current EU states belong to EMU. Still, it appears to conflict somewhat with the potential for economic and monetary governance across Europe. Because the EU's responsibilities in the areas of macroeconomic and fiscal policy are restricted, there is a certain tension between macroeconomic and fiscal policies, which are only partially coordinated, and a unified monetary policy for all EMU states. Rapidly growing EMU membership in the future may further aggravate some of the pressures stemming from this imbalance. However, in spite of these tensions, the institutional foundations of EMU are stable, as are those of the EU, and seem so far to be capable of absorbing various economic or political pressures. Hence, the scenario of an actual breakdown of EMU is unlikely. Tensions will certainly persist, however, and possibly affect ECB policymaking in the future. The clear focus of the ECB on price-level stability and its general performance in the years since its creation, however, indicate that monetary union in Europe, in spite of the partially political rationales that have led to its creation, is a sound endeavor. Hence, it is indeed likely that the euro will gradually assume a more important role in global economic and financial affairs.

If the ECB is able to maintain the orientation of its general policies in the future, the euro may, due to increasing international use, become a competitor of currently existing global currencies. It would only become a true rival of other currencies, notably the US dollar, however, if the ECB's policies were to be determined by political demands. Institutional provisions shielding the ECB from various forms of day-to-day political interference, despite voices pleading for it to assume a more proactive macroeconomic policy stance, prevent Europe's new central bank, for example, from implementing an active exchange-rate policy. The ECB is unlikely to ever turn into a politically driven entity. But it is likely to enhance its significance as the monetary locus for Europe and neighboring states, and to increase its role in global economic and monetary affairs.

In order to describe in more detail the euro's origins, current state, and prospects, and to illustrate some links between political and economic forces in the creation of EMU, this book addresses several topics in sequence. It begins with a chapter on the history of European monetary integration to set the stage to the rest of the book. Subsequent chapters illustrate the transition from the EMS to EMU, give an overview of the institutional structure of EMU, discuss aspects of fiscal and monetary performance in Europe, and describe current and possible future effects of the euro. Each chapter addresses specific aspects within this general context.

Chapter 2 illustrates how the Bretton Woods system, set up in the aftermath of World War II, aimed at stabilizing international monetary and financial relations and preventing a repetition of the competitive currency devaluations that occurred during the interwar period. A main goal of the new Bretton Woods institutions—notably the International Monetary Fund (IMF) and the International Bank for Reconstruction and Development (IBRD)—was to avoid the outbreak of another deep global economic depression. In practice, in the framework of the Bretton Woods system, the US dollar had gradually developed into the anchor currency of international monetary relations. The currencies of western European states were embedded in this international system of fixed, but adjustable, exchange rates.

The breakdown of the Bretton Woods system in August 1971, however, led Western European states to consider a regional monetary system that could shield their economies against adverse effects of international currency volatility. The currency "Snake" was set up in an attempt to create a common float vis-à-vis the US dollar. Plans for the establishment of an actual monetary union in Western Europe by 1980, however, proved to be premature. The 1970s were difficult years in terms of international economic and monetary conditions: the two oil-price shocks and subsequent economic recession led to increased speculative pressures on currencies of European Community (EC) states, including the French franc. Due to economic and monetary pressures on many participating states, the Snake gradually turned into an extended German-mark zone. Toward the end of the 1970s, a new, somewhat more modest plan for a regional monetary system materialized. It was supported by prominent political actors such as Helmut Schmidt, then chancellor of Germany; the president of France, Valéry Giscard d'Estaing; and Roy Jenkins, then president of the European Commission.

Economic exigencies of the time, in addition to currency volatility in international markets, led to intensified demands for European monetary unification. In 1979, the EMS was established as a comparatively far-reaching regime of European monetary cooperation that kept the fluctuation margins among European currencies within narrow bands, although not tied to international currencies such as the US dollar. The EMS did not establish the institutional foundations, such as a supranational central bank, for a monetary union. Instead it built a structure for monetary cooperation in which central banks would be obliged to maintain the predetermined margins within which their domestic currencies were allowed to move. This system was quite effective for most of the 1980s and 1990s, although it experienced some significant currency turmoil (notably in 1992 and 1993). Some analysts view the harmonization and common decrease of inflation rates (the rate of annual price-level increases), as well as long-term interest rates, as primarily due to the very existence of the EMS,[4] whereas others explain the harmonization as a result of the convergence of monetary policy ideas among political and economic elites.[5] An especially impressive common lowering of interest rates among EMS states in the second half of the 1980s reinforced optimistic expectations during the negotiations on the Treaty on European Union (TEU) that monetary union, based on predefined convergence criteria, would indeed be an economically and politically feasible option for Europe.

Chapter 2 also presents the structure and modes of operation of the EMS in more detail, since the EMS can be viewed as the actual precursor to the current EMU. The system consisted of two major elements: the Exchange Rate Mechanism (ERM) and the European Currency Unit (ECU). The ECU had been designed to develop into a new unit of account for the EC member states, but it never played this role in reality. The chapter also explains how the ECU constituted a basket currency and describes its composition in terms of the participating domestic currencies. A bilateral parity grid was set up, indicating the limits that central banks could tolerate within the ERM regarding exchange-rate variability among domestic currencies. The official exchange rates between the domestic currencies and the ECU—the central rates within the EMS—were determined on the basis of intergovernmental agreement in the Council of Ministers of Economics and Finance (Ecofin Council). Day-to-day exchange rates, however, were determined by market forces. Central banks in each of the participating member states were obliged to intervene in the financial markets to defend the parity of these rates. Official reserves were not actually pooled, but a system was in effect to facilitate both short- and long-term lending among the central banks of EMS member states.

The first years of the EMS were marked by relatively frequent realignments, that is, changes in official (central) exchange rates between the ECU and selected national currencies.[6] The German mark and the Dutch guilder, especially, were strong currencies in the system and appreciated in value as compared to other currencies (such as the Italian lira and French franc). The chapter describes the role of the German Bundesbank in the system, its independence from politics, and the credibility of its anti-inflationary monetary policy. By the end of the 1980s, the frequency of realignments within the EMS decreased significantly, a sign of the stability and success of this regional monetary cooperation scheme. Moreover, both a lowering and a convergence of inflation rates were observed for several EC member states. The EMS was shaken, however, by significant currency turbulence in 1992 and 1993.

Chapter 3 describes the transition from the EMS and the developments leading to the actual creation of EMU. In the framework of the 1986 Single European Act (SEA), EC member states had already achieved the conditions necessary for the completion of an internal market. Two basic elements of this plan were the new principle of mutual recognition of regulations (national product regulations, for example) instead of harmonization and the liberalized flow of persons, goods, services, and capital across the borders of EC states. By July 1990, the first stage of EMU—still within the internal market program—became effective. It mainly encompassed the abolition of remaining capital controls among EC member states, controls that were decisive earlier, for example, for European countries seeking to avoid extensive capital outflows or inflows that might lead to an undesired effect on the value of their domestic currency. Intensive discussions, partially based on different theoretical explanations regarding the role of economic and monetary policies in processes of regional integration, accompanied the move toward the creation of the internal market. Is a common market desirable and sustainable without monetary union? Could more benefits be achieved by adopting a common currency among EC states, mainly due to price transparency and a reduction of transaction costs? Should a European monetary union be envisioned, or would it be preferable to let the EC integration project stop at the establishment of a common market? Disagreement on such issues existed in public opinion, among academics and monetary experts, and among government representatives alike. For example, the British government under Margaret Thatcher opposed the creation of EMU altogether, at least before the actual intergovernmental negotiations on EMU began. But domestically, not least within her own Conservative party, significant internal opposition to her policy stance on European integration issues contributed to pressures to transfer leadership of the Conservative party from herself to John Major.

By comparison, the governments of Germany and France clearly supported the plan to establish EMU, although they held different preferences and put different emphases on particular aspects of the project.[7] EMU was perceived by a majority of EC governments as a scheme that would increase price transparency within Europe, help curtail transaction costs (for example, the costs associated with exchanging national currencies), and contribute to the achievement of economies of scale (essentially gains resulting from a bigger market and production on a larger scale). The provisions on EMU contained in the TEU foresaw a certain harmonization of macroeconomic and monetary performance of EC member states before EMU would start.[8] Accordingly, the Maastricht Treaty (the TEU) defined five convergence criteria with the aim of achieving more convergence regarding inflation rates, (long-term) interest rates, government deficits, government debt, and exchange-rate variability. The actual plan for monetary union as contained in the TEU foresaw a move toward EMU in three stages.[9] A major element of the second stage would be the introduction of the European Monetary Institute (EMI) in Frankfurt, Germany. The EMI would be a predecessor of the ECB and an institution to monitor the convergence of macroeconomic and monetary policies of EC member states. Chapter 3 also describes the launch of EMU on January 1, 1999, and shows the patterns according to which exchange rates between the euro and its national currencies became irrevocably fixed.

The institutional structure of the European System of Central Banks (ESCB) and of the ECB is discussed in Chapter 4. The chapter provides an overview of the ESCB and the composition and responsibilities of the ECB's governing council, executive board, and general council. In addition, it discusses some of the challenges for these institutions stemming from enlargement and related processes.

The ESCB is composed of the ECB and the central banks of all EU member states. By comparison, the Eurosystem comprises the ECB and the central banks of EU states participating in EMU. Since membership in the EU and EMU is not congruent (see Table 1.1), EU states not participating in the Eurosystem are ESCB members with a special status. With EU expansion to twenty-five members in May 2004, the number of central banks in the ESCB (but not yet in the Eurosystem) has considerably increased.

Europe's new central bank, the ECB, is governed by a governing council and an executive board. The ECB executive board comprises a president and vice-president and four other monetary policy experts. The first ECB president was Willem Duisenberg, formerly head of the Dutch central bank. Jean-Claude Trichet, former head of the central bank of France, became the second president. Members of the ECB executive board are assumed to defend a "euro-area perspective" within EMU and to avoid bias regarding the economic or monetary exigencies of their own states. Among the major responsibilities of the executive board are the implementation of EMU monetary policies according to the overall guidelines set by the ECB governing council, the determination of EMU-wide interest rates, and the formulation of respective instructions to the national central banks within the ESCB.

The ECB governing council is composed of the six members of the ECB's executive board and the heads of the central banks of all Eurosystem states (that is, of central banks of EU states participating in EMU). Among the main tasks of the governing council are the formulation of monetary policy for the euro area, including decisions on key interest rates; promotion of a smooth operation of payments systems; and the holding and managing of official reserves of the Eurosystem states.

The new EU states as of May 2004 are full members of the ECB's general council. Once they become members of EMU, however, the ECB governing council will adapt its modes of voting and decision-making. The different possibilities for institutional reform and the option finally to be implemented in view of enlargement are also discussed in Chapter 4. The ECB has a clear statutory mandate to maintain price stability in the euro area. However, the chapter briefly addresses the relationship between the ECB and the Ecofin Council, as is defined to some extent in the provisions of the TEU, regarding potential political influence on exchange-rate policy in the euro area. Regarding possible participation of EMU states in exchange-rate schemes, the chapter distinguishes between the potential leverage of political forces regarding formal and more informal forms of multilateral exchange-rate agreements. The chapter describes the nature of the "ERM II," seen for the most part as a tool to prepare new EU states for later EMU membership by establishing fluctuation margins for domestic currencies around the euro. Finally, the chapter explains why some EU states— Denmark, Sweden, and the United Kingdom—are not currently members of EMU and illustrates dilemmas in this regard in domestic politics, for example in the United Kingdom. It also shows prospects for new EU states to join EMU. Chapter 4 focuses on the relationship of some non-EU states, notably Switzerland and Norway, with EMU and the euro.

Chapter 5 addresses an issue at the heart of many discussions on EMU: the fiscal implications of monetary integration and repercussions on EMU states' macroeconomic performance. Of the five convergence criteria embedded in the TEU, EU states found it especially difficult to comply with the fiscal criteria regarding government deficits and debts, in part because most of them faced economic recession in the beginning of the 1990s. In order to ensure that member states would aim to conduct responsible fiscal policies, also after EMU would have started, the Stability and Growth Pact (SGP) was introduced in June 1997. However, the SGP was often criticized; while it provided clear political guidelines regarding fiscal performance, it was not entirely convincing in economic terms. The SGP foresaw sanctioning mechanisms for member states exceeding the criteria, notably regarding ratios of budget deficits and government debt to GDP. After the start of EMU, several EU states had difficulty complying with the fiscal criteria.

It is difficult to satisfy the provisions of the SGP, especially in times of economic downturn. When an economy shrinks, it is important to provide stimulation, not least by means of governmental investment measures. However, the SGP constrains public expenditures. Allowing EMU members to run large budget deficits risked creating collective action problems within the euro area; budget deficits may induce inflationary pressures and possibly lead to an increase in interest rates for the euro area. The SGP was established to provide a surveillance mechanism that would, through the European Commission, monitor and, if necessary, sanction government behavior. Generally, incumbent governments tend to increase public spending before elections in order to increase chances for electoral success. Clearly, the SGP, and EMU more generally, constrain this option. Within EMU, decisions on monetary policy are now delegated to the ECB, and governments have little leeway regarding domestic monetary, and to some extent macroeconomic, policies.[10] Tools to steer the domestic economy have therefore shifted from monetary to fiscal policy instruments. EU governments are generally reluctant to pool sovereignty in the domain of fiscal policy, however, possibly due to the very inability to directly influence monetary policies affecting their domestic economies. As a result, a gap exists within EMU between the pooling of sovereignty in the realm of monetary policy within the ECB and the fact that competencies in the fiscal domain rest mostly with individual EU member states. In essence, the SGP aimed to provide a tool to control government behavior within EMU in order to increase prospects for long-term EMU stability, but its provisions were difficult to meet.

With several EU states having difficulty complying with the criteria of the SGP, the pact faced increased criticism. Ireland and Portugal, for example, received warnings from the European Commission regarding their fiscal performance. They then introduced measures to comply with the SGP's provisions. By comparison, the government of France, having received similar warnings, signaled unwillingness to adapt its domestic fiscal policy. With Germany also unable to comply with the SGP criteria, notably the one on the budget-deficit ceiling of 3 percent of GDP, the pact came into troubled waters. Moreover, it was criticized by academics for being inflexible and implying a risk of generating economically counterproductive effects.[11]

Chapter 6 focuses on prospects for the euro's future: What could the possible repercussions of the euro be on the international monetary system? What might be the effects of EU and EMU enlargement by several new members? Is the euro a rival to other world currencies, notably the US dollar? Accordingly, Chapter 6 discusses prospects for the euro in global financial and monetary affairs. It analyzes the ECB's emphasis on price stability and patterns of macroeconomic and monetary convergence within EMU. It discusses ECB policies and factors affecting the credibility of a currency in international financial affairs. Finally, it addresses the possible role of the euro in international monetary affairs, as a unit of account, a means of payment, or a store of value. On the basis of this analysis, the chapter contends that, mainly due to the ECB's emphasis on price stability, the euro may indeed be used increasingly in global transactions, for example, to denominate trade and as a store of value (in both private and official use). The EU's weight in the global economy and in global trade relations combined with political stability, seem to strengthen the role of EMU's new currency. In addition, the ECB's independence from politics may be conducive to long-term economic-growth perspectives in the euro area. However, voices within the EU and EMU express the desire that the ECB, in spite of its strict price-stability mandate, put more emphasis on a growth-oriented monetary policy. It is unclear at this time whether these voices will gain strength in the future, but such a shift in emphasis would clearly run counter to the ECB's policy of price stability.

As this book illustrates, there have been several attempts in Europe, even before the start of EMU, not only to integrate markets, but also to establish a monetary union. These attempts have often been hampered, however, by member states' reluctance to give up monetary sovereignty, on the one hand, and by international developments constraining the capacity of European governments to integrate in the monetary realm on the other hand. Processes of globalization may have increased pressures to integrate monetary policy making in Europe, but often these very pressures, along with adverse international economic and monetary conditions, rendered the path toward European monetary union difficult in practice.

There has been significant skepticism, in public opinion as well as among economists and monetary experts, as to whether monetary union is feasible and sustainable in Europe. This skepticism was shared by prominent academics, several of whom viewed the project as simply premature. From an economic perspective, the main criticism raised is that the EU does not (yet) constitute an Optimum Currency Area (OCA) in that it does not have a degree of labor mobility and wage flexibility that would allow a relatively low-risk transition to monetary union. However, the establishment of EMU on January 1, 1999, has illustrated that monetary union in the EU was certainly feasible in a technical sense, even if it constituted a largely politically driven project. In fact, the introduction of the euro during the course of 2002 amounted to what might be judged to be a technical and logistical masterpiece.

Almost all EU states joined EMU at the beginning, and many more states are to join the project in the future. There still are critical voices questioning whether the introduction of EMU, and of the euro, constituted a good idea after all. As several observers have stated, EMU is not a natural development, occurring purely on the basis of economic logic, but a deliberate (political) effort of EU governments to push forward and strengthen the EU integration process.[12] This book contends that EMU may indeed largely be a political enterprise, but the ECB has shown an impressive degree of adherence to its price-stability mandate. It remains refreshingly independent of political forces and undoubtedly constitutes an increasingly strong and visible actor in today's global financial and monetary relations.

Notes

1. Discussions on the feasibility and probability of the creation of EMU are now closed, which may still leave academics to reflect about the feasibility, sustainability, and consequences of the project. On this, see Jones (2002).

2. This topic is discussed, for example, in Henning (1996), Portes and Rey (1998), Collignon and Mundschenk (1999), and Henning and Padoan (2000).

3. See Jones (2002).

4. See Walsh (2000).

5. See McNamara (1998).

6. See Tsoukalis (1999).

7. See Hosli (2000).

8. Data on policy preferences of various EC governments on EMU, along with those of representatives of EC institutions, are given in Kugler and Williams (1994). For preferences of EU governments and adaptations during the negotiation process, see Moravcsik (1998) or Dyson and Featherstone (1999).

9. For a detailed overview of the various provisions foreseen in the TEU in order to complete monetary union, see Flowers and Lees (2002) or Neal and Barbezat (1998).

10. In fact, the delegation of monetary policy authority to an independent central bank may reduce tensions within governments, since potentially conflictive debates on monetary policy are taken out of the context of domestic politics. See Bernhard and Leblang (2002).

11. For a discussion of the rigidity of the SGP's fiscal criteria and suggestions for improvement, see Begg (2002) or De Grauwe (2003). On the SGP's provisions, and criticisms raised against the pact more generally, see Leblond (2003) or Heipertz and Verdun (2004).

12. See Moravcsik (1998) or Tsoukalis (1999).

2

The Snake and
the European Monetary System

Ａs World War II came to an end, politicians of the major industrialized democracies aimed to set up a new system of global economic and monetary governance that would allow for sustainable prosperity and peace. On the basis of results achieved at a conference held in Bretton Woods, New Hampshire, in July 1944, the Bretton Woods system—with its two major institutions, the IMF and the World Bank—came into existence.[1] In the absence of modern techniques, such as good microphones, well-designed meeting rooms, and sophisticated translating capacities, the negotiations among delegates of forty-five countries took place under fairly difficult circumstances. Communication among the participants, including representatives from Russia,[2] was a true logistical and political challenge.

Different perspectives prevailed among the major negotiating parties regarding desired patterns of global monetary governance. The United Kingdom, represented by John Maynard Keynes, favored an encompassing role for the IMF, taking over functions of what essentially amounts to a global central bank, whereas the US delegation supported a distinctively more moderate approach to global monetary governance. But several representatives shared a belief that the world was in need of a managed global monetary order. A system of fixed exchange rates was preferred—in light of the rather disastrous experiences with floating exchange rates in the 1930s—and viewed as the most stable and most beneficial basis for the development of mutually advantageous trade relations.[3] Practices such as competitive devaluation, it was generally agreed, should be avoided, since they had been seriously restricting investment flows and had damaged international trade relations during the 1930s.[4]

The General Agreement on Tariffs and Trade (GATT) was also set up in the framework of the Bretton Woods system. Originally, plans existed to also create an International Trade Organization (ITO) with a wider scope than the mere reduction of tariffs, but this treaty failed to be ratified, notably due to opposition in the US Congress. Hence, patterns of global monetary and commercial governance within the Bretton Woods system were somewhat lopsided, with monetary regimes being further developed than trade regimes.

The postwar objectives of the IMF, according to the agreements reached at Bretton Woods, were to restore global exchange-rate stability and to provide a sound basis for the development of peaceful international economic exchanges. IMF member states, mainly advanced industrialized economies, declared a par value of their domestic currency in terms of both the US dollar and gold. Gold reserves could be freely exchanged against US dollars, generally at the price of 35 US dollars per ounce of gold. In addition, the IMF aimed to encourage unrestricted conversion of member states' currencies. In the framework of the Bretton Woods system, member-state currencies could fluctuate against the US dollar by plus or minus 1 percent. However, after consultation with the IMF, the dollar parity of participating currencies could be modified. In the early years of the Bretton Woods system, par values were adapted quite frequently.[5]

Starting in 1948, Marshall-Plan funding was channeled into Europe through the Organization for European Economic Cooperation (OEEC), later renamed the Organization for Economic Cooperation and Development (OECD), to help reduce the huge balance-of-payments deficits of European countries. In 1950, under the surveillance of the OEEC, a European Payments Union (EUP) was established with the aim of clearing intra-European payments on a multilateral basis. Gradually, policymakers also supported the view that avoiding currency volatility and narrowing fluctuation bands among European currencies would be beneficial to prospects for intra-European trade.

In 1958, the European Monetary Agreement (EMA) was set up, essentially replacing the EUP. Within this new system, European Economic Community (EEC) states agreed to limit the fluctuation margins of their domestic currencies against the US dollar to plus or minus 0.75 percent. This constituted a reduction of the prevalent margins applicable in the Bretton Woods system. Heisenberg (1999: 22) explains the major reason for this step: floating of a currency with plus or minus 1 percent against the US dollar implied a possible floating of four times that margin—4 percent—as compared to another European currency.

The new provisions according to the EMA, by comparison, constrained bilateral fluctuation margins to a maximum of four times 0.75 (that is, 3) percent. This measure was expected to facilitate exchanges within the EEC, including those related to its new agricultural policy.

Based on a provision contained in the Treaty of Rome, in 1964 a Committee of Central Bank Governors (CCBG), composed of the governors of EEC states' central banks, was set up to encourage central-bank cooperation among the members. By allowing a member of the European Commission and the chairman of the EEC Monetary Committee to attend CCBG meetings, moreover, a formal link with EEC institutions was established.[6] Among the major goals of the CCBG was the coordination of member states' monetary policies, with the overall aim of increasing price stability. The establishment of the EMS in 1979 increased the importance of the CCBG. The committee was dissolved, however, at the start of stage two of EMU on January 1, 1994, and was replaced by the Council of the EMI—the actual precursor of the ECB.[7]

The Bretton Woods system, in general terms, relied on confidence in the US dollar. It depended on the strength of the US economy, the availability of a large amount of US gold reserves, and an unequivocal commitment on the part of the United States to convert dollars into gold.[8] Partially due to the very success of the postwar management of global monetary and trade relations, however, there was an ongoing outflow of US dollars from the United States. Generally, the US trade deficit and foreign holdings of US dollars provided a sufficient degree of liquidity for international commercial and monetary transactions. If the trade deficit should grow, however, and the outstanding dollar holdings outside the United States become too large compared to existing gold reserves, confidence in the US dollar, and thus in the Bretton Woods system, could be jeopardized.[9] The potential seriousness of this problem was emphasized by Robert Triffin.[10]

By the end of 1959, due to a significant economic upturn, European and Japanese official reserves, held for a large part in US dollars, equaled those of the United States. In 1960, for the first time, holdings of US dollars outside the United States exceeded US gold reserves.[11] Patterns of gradually increasing financial interdependence, however, generated pressures on both national and international monetary governance. Significant international capital flows complicated effective domestic responses to global monetary developments. As a result, the United States gradually abdicated international monetary leadership. In essence, it started pursuing a policy of benign neglect: an approach characterized by an emphasis on domestic policy priorities, regardless of pressures stemming from the international monetary system, and a rather passive stance regarding options for global monetary reform.[12] On August 15, 1971, US President Richard Nixon reacted to pressures stemming from increasing imbalances between US gold reserves and the international role of the dollar and unilaterally renounced the convertibility of the US dollar to gold.[13] With this, the Bretton Woods system essentially collapsed.

In general terms, uncertainties related to a fluctuating exchange rate tend to be more tolerable for larger, less trade-dependent countries, including the United States.[14] By comparison, EEC states, characterized by trade dependence and based on open economies (that is, having large shares of imports and exports as compared to GDP), had to find ways to avoid the potentially detrimental effects on their commercial and economic relations generated by exchange-rate volatility among their national currencies. A central idea regarding the containment of possible currency volatility—a phenomenon potentially disruptive also for the Common Agricultural Policy (CAP)—was a new scheme of regional exchange-rate stability. With interdependent economies, economic pressures could contain a risk that governments, especially in times of economic downturn, might aim for competitive currency devaluations. Clearly, this would be detrimental to prospects for the European integration project.

In December 1971, in the course of the breakup of the Bretton Woods system, the ten then largest world economies reached the Smithsonian agreement (the "Basel Agreement"). The principal component of this agreement was a widening of the fluctuation margins of their currencies against the US dollar as compared to the Bretton Woods system. Parity values against the US dollar were adapted and fluctuation margins widened from plus or minus 1 percent to plus or minus 2.25 percent (resulting in an overall possible fluctuation band of 4.5 percent).[15] As a consequence of this arrangement, intra-European exchange rates could vary by as much as 9 percent. Considering the potentially detrimental effects of this scheme on intra-EC trade, new avenues were explored to limit intra-European currency fluctuation.

In March 1972, the "Snake-in-the-Tunnel" regime was created.[16] States participating in the Snake were Belgium, France, Germany, Italy, Luxembourg, and the Netherlands. Essentially, the Snake set bilateral fluctuation margins for all participating EC currencies of plus or minus 2.25 percent. Simultaneously, these participating currencies were allowed to fluctuate within a margin of 6 percent within the tunnel of the US dollar. On May 1, 1972, with the prospect of forthcoming EC membership, the United Kingdom and Denmark joined the Snake. Norway became an associated member on May 23, 1972.[17]

In 1973, however, the first oil-price crisis put a major strain on the Snake. The ensuing economic recession, moreover, forced several EC states to either drastically adapt their monetary policies or to leave the Snake regime. Many European states suffered a loss of competitiveness due to the first OPEC oil-price shock and the dollar's decline after 1973 (which tended to favor US exporting interests). Foreign interventions, as well as domestic policy adjustments, remained rather limited, however, and were unable to contain the strong pressures on prevailing exchange rates.[18] The United Kingdom withdrew from the Snake in June 1972, Italy in February 1973, and Denmark in June 1973 (although Denmark reentered the regime later). The Smithsonian tunnel collapsed in 1973, but the Snake was maintained nonetheless. Once the orientation toward the US dollar was given up, the Snake had lost its tunnel. The floating version of the Snake was subsequently humorously referred to as "the Snake in the Lake."[19]

France withdrew from the Snake in January 1974, rejoining it in July of 1975.[20] But nonconvergence in terms of macroeconomic policies forced France to leave the Snake again in 1976.[21] At the end of the 1970s, the Snake represented little more than an extended German-mark zone, with only Germany, Denmark, and the Benelux countries remaining as members. Apart from the adverse economic conditions under which the Snake had operated, especially the sharp economic recession of the mid-1970s, the EC states held differing views regarding appropriate responses to macroeconomic disturbances. They therefore reacted in different ways to the economic and financial strains of the 1970s. The German Bundesbank, for example, adopted a strategy that was focused primarily on stemming potential inflation due to increasing oil prices. By comparison, France opted to use an expansion of fiscal measures, aiming to stimulate the economy and to combat unemployment.

New pressures on exchange rates emerged, not least due to massive international currency flows. The Smithsonian agreement had been intended as a temporary construct, providing participating states time to negotiate long-term reform of the global monetary system. In fact, the agreement mostly provided temporary crisis control. By March 1973, all major world currencies were floating.[22]

Stabilization of exchange rates was difficult to achieve within the EC, especially considering external pressures on the domestic monetary policies of the EC member states. The Snake was a relatively modest endeavor compared to some broader and more far-reaching ideas regarding monetary cooperation in Europe. In 1970, the Werner Plan—named after the then prime minister of Luxembourg—had called for the establishment of a European monetary union within a decade. The plan foresaw three stages in reaching this goal—stages similar to the more recent steps contained in the respective provisions of the TEU. But the project turned out to be premature and unfeasible mainly due to adverse economic conditions, notably the oil-price shocks and the accompanying recessions of the 1970s.

Discussions about how to achieve monetary union in Europe were generally dominated by two opposing schools of thought. "Monetarists" advocated an irrevocable fixing of exchange rates as a tool to promote economic convergence among EC member states. By comparison, "economists" favored macroeconomic convergence in preparation for an ultimate fixing of exchange rates. Among the major proponents of the monetarist view were government representatives of France, Italy, and Belgium, and among those supporting the economist approach were the governments of Germany and the Netherlands.[23]

In view of external pressures on the steering of domestic economies, it was difficult for some EC states to stay within even a modest, pragmatic approach to regional exchange-rate stability such as the Snake. In addition, some currencies experienced relatively strong pressures to appreciate within the system, whereas others were forced to depreciate or even to leave the system entirely.

Most notably, the German mark faced pressure to appreciate within the Snake regime. Similarly, the currency of nonmember of the Snake (and even of the EC), Switzerland, also faced strong upward pressures. For both Germany and Switzerland, however, an appreciating currency was an unfavorable option: both countries have sizeable export industries that would be hurt economically by a high relative value of their domestic currencies. By comparison, the governments of France, Italy, and the United Kingdom devalued their currencies in response to pressures from the financial markets.

Nonetheless, a convergence of EC governments' views on how to conduct monetary policy gradually materialized. According to Kathleen McNamara (1998, 1999), the critical factor for progress regarding European monetary integration, beginning in the mid-1970s and solidifying in the 1980s, was a process of "ideational convergence" regarding the conduct of macroeconomic and monetary policy. In several EC states, the Keynesian beliefs of political elites were gradually replaced by a neoliberal policy consensus. As a consequence, the pursuit of price stability was put ahead of goals such as economic growth or full employment. McNamara views this as the major explanation for the downward convergence in inflation rates across Europe.[24] In a similar vein, Sandholtz (1993) has argued that an emerging monetary-policy consensus was at the core of the increased monetary integration in the EC.

Indeed, it has not always been an intellectual consensus that monetary policy should be directed toward the maintenance of price stability.[25] Since the 1970s, however, economists and central bankers have shared the opinion that Keynesian policies of demand management, and the Phillips curve in particular, were essentially discredited. The Phillips curve posited that, in the long run, an inverse relationship existed between inflation and unemployment: a country could only achieve lower unemployment in exchange for higher inflation.[26] Accordingly, monetary-policy reasoning prior to the 1970s predicted a relatively stable trade-off between inflation and unemployment, but theoretical critiques and empirical evidence increasingly undermined confidence in this belief.[27] More generally, since the end of World War II, theoretical developments have frequently affected practical applications in monetary policy making, and conversely, empirical findings have induced adaptations, or even led to the abandonment, of monetary-policy theories (including theories on exchange-rate movements).[28] Surely, the convergence of ideas regarding monetary policies also significantly affected prospects for European monetary union.[29]

The consensus that monetary policy should be oriented primarily toward the goal of price stability appears to partially collapse, however, when policymakers have to make more specific decisions about the extent of economic growth prospects they are willing to sacrifice in exchange for a small risk of inflation. Hence, monetary-policy consensus is less pronounced when it comes to the degree to which states are willing to accept inflation risks and to subordinate other economic policy objectives to these risks.[30] To a certain extent, this topic may still divide members within some European institutions, including the ECB governing council.

In institutional terms, the Snake was established, for the most part, as a symmetric system, partially in response to French objections to the prominent role of the US dollar in the Bretton Woods system. But after the Snake regime had been freed from its Smithsonian tunnel, it was the German mark that became Europe's key currency and anti-inflationary anchor. In essence, there were hardly any mechanisms through which other EC states could influence monetary-policy decisions of the Bundesbank. This accountability deficit, in addition to adverse international economic circumstances, may have posed the ultimate obstacle to the success of the Snake.[31] In spite of the German mark's prominent role, however, the history of European monetary cooperation has been marked by friction between the Bundesbank and the German federal government, especially regarding the potential international dimensions of the Bundesbank's policies.[32]

Calls for stronger monetary convergence among EC states were frequent in the second half of the 1970s, despite the various challenges the Snake's member states were experiencing. The president of the European Commission, Roy Jenkins, had in fact advocated schemes of enhanced currency stability for the EC soon after the start of the Snake. Moreover, Helmut Schmidt, then German chancellor, and Valery Giscard d'Estaing, president of France, called for the establishment of a new regime to moderate potential exchange-rate variability among the currencies of EC states. These central political actors tended to work through bilateral rather than multilateral methods and usually met outside the EC's institutional framework. However, discussions between France and Germany regarding increased monetary integration in Europe often included other prospective participants of a new European exchange-rate regime, notably Belgium, Italy, and the Netherlands.[33] In 1978, an EC summit meeting in The Hague officially sanctioned the plan to create a new European monetary regime. The EMS was inaugurated in March 1979.[34]

The EMS was designed to resemble the Snake in the tunnel but, most importantly, it would involve only the currencies of the EC member states. The US dollar would not serve as a focal point, or anchor, in the system. The EMS contained two major elements: the ERM and the ECU. The ERM established a grid of bilateral parities in which currencies were allowed to fluctuate within a margin of plus or minus 2.25 percent around their bilateral central rates. The national central banks were obliged to intervene when currencies reached their fluctuation margins: the ERM included a 75-percent divergence intervention threshold determining when central banks should intervene to support the value of a currency.[35] A European Monetary Cooperation Fund (EMCF) had already been established in the framework of the Snake in April 1972. With the EMS, however, the borrowing facilities of the EMCF were extended to enable national central banks to effectively intervene in financial markets.

The domestic currencies of the EC member states were to be incorporated into a new EC unit of account, the ECU.[36] In essence, the ECU was set up according to the model of Special Drawing Rights (SDR), as created by the IMF in 1969.[37] Daily ECU exchange rates fluctuated according to market pressures.[38] Table 2.1 provides examples of such daily market rates for two randomly chosen days in 1996: January 24 and February 21.

Table 2.1 shows how, within a period of less than thirty days, the value of some international currencies, including the US dollar and the Japanese yen, depreciated slightly as compared to EMS currencies. Some EMS currencies, such as the Greek drachma, the French franc, the Irish punt, and the Portuguese escudo, also experienced a moderate decrease in the external value of their domestic currencies. Variations within short time periods were usually not extensive, but if fluctuations proved to be of a serious magnitude, ERM central rates could be adapted. This option reflected the principle of "fixed but adjustable" exchange rates.

Bilateral exchange rates between the ECU and the domestic currencies—the EMS central rates—were agreed upon in the framework of the Ecofin Council. The weights of the national currencies in the ECU bas-

Table 2.1 Value of the ECU Expressed in Different Currencies (January 24, 1996 and February 21, 1996)

National Currency	January 24, 1996	February 21, 1996
US dollar (USD)	1.28013	1.29594
Japanese yen (YEN)	135.156	136.812
Swiss franc (SFR)	1.51759	1.53828
Belgian franc (BLF)	38.7942	38.7842
Danish krone (DKR)	7.30248	7.29160
German mark (DM)	1.88691	1.88533
Greek drachma (DRA)	311.532	311.932
Spanish peseta (PTA)	159.120	158.895
French franc (FF)	6.46528	6.49784
Irish punt (IRL)	0.814796	0.817318
Italian lira (LIT)	2045.41	2040.97
Dutch guilder (HFL)	2.11298	2.11121
Austrian schilling (ÖS)	13.2685	13.2613
Portuguese escudo (ESC)	195.603	196.672
Finnish markka (FMK)	5.79001	5.85311
Swedish krone (SKR)	8.77527	8.77519
British pound sterling (UKL)	0.845247	0.841519
Norwegian krone (NKR)	8.27602	8.24800

ket were to be revised every five years. Such general revisions of central rates were conducted in both 1984 and 1989. In between these five-year revisions, however, market pressures on some EMS currencies caused a series of realignments. The respective new bilateral central rates were agreed upon by the Ecofin Council.

In the framework of the five-year revisions inducing a reweighting of the official ECU, and the several realignments in between, shares of the strongest currencies in the system—and hence their respective contributions to the ECU basket—would have steadily increased had there not been a corrective tool. Table 2.2 provides an overview of the weights of currencies in the ECU basket as they applied starting in September 1989.

The German mark, the French franc, the Dutch guilder, and the British pound sterling—the latter not being in the ERM—held the largest shares in the ECU basket.[39] When a currency appreciated, its percentage share in the basket, which was based on a fixed weight, increased in the absence of realignment. The converse held for depreciating currencies.

In order to avoid speculative attacks, ECU central rates were frozen with the entry into force of the TEU.[40] Hence, since the ratification of the TEU in 1993, the weights of the national currencies in the ECU basket remained stable. Evidently, every time central rates were adapted, capital gains and losses could occur. Investors holding ECU bonds, for

Table 2.2 Composition of the ECU Basket (September 21, 1989)

German mark	0.6242
French franc	1.332
Dutch guilder	0.2198
Belgian franc	3.301
Luxembourg franc	0.13
Italian lira	151.8
Danish krone	0.1976
Irish punt	0.008552
British pound sterling	0.08784
Greek drachma	1.44
Spanish peseta	6.885
Portuguese escudo	1.393

Source: Eurostat, ECU-EMS Information and Central Bank Interest Rates, November 1995, p. 10.

example, could be negatively affected when the weight of a strong currency decreased.

Institutionally, the EMS was designed as a symmetric system. The ECU central rates were determined on the basis of agreement between EMS member states, and all participating members were obligated to intervene to defend bilateral exchange-rate parities. In practice, the system—like the Snake before it—was dominated by one player: the Bundesbank.[41] The Bundesbank set its monetary policy rather autonomously, whereas the central banks of other EMS member states were essentially forced to follow its decisions. Among the reasons the Bundesbank was able to exert this power were its full independence from political pressures and its credibility as regards price stability (supported by a profound aversion, shared by the German public on the basis of traumatic experiences of the interwar period, to excessive inflation rates).

New EC member states usually joined the EMS as well, but some waited before actually acceding to the ERM. Spain joined the ERM in 1989, for example, the United Kingdom in 1990, and Portugal in 1992.[42] But after extensive speculative attacks on their domestic currencies, Finland, Italy, and the United Kingdom withdrew from the ERM in September 1992. Shortly thereafter, the Spanish, Portuguese, and Irish currencies were forced to devalue. Subsequently, in the summer of 1993, the French franc was almost forced to withdraw from the ERM. These pressures on currency markets finally led to a political compromise within the EU on a widening of the ERM fluctuation margins, to plus and minus 15 percent. Hence, in essence, domestic currencies were almost floating.

In the late 1980s, the relative stability of the EMS contributed to a phase of general "Euro-optimism," reinforced on the economic front by positive accounts regarding the economic potential of the new single European market. This positive mood was further reinforced by an economic upturn, which preceded the economic recession of the early 1990s. In the late 1980s, monetary integration in the EU appeared to be feasible in the medium-term future. This optimistic mood was supported by analyses conducted by the European Commission on additional economic gains to be achieved by monetary union, including one of the most decisive contributions, the Commission's published study titled "One Market, One Money."[43]

In 1988, the European Council appointed a special committee to explore concrete steps that might result in the realization of European monetary union. This committee was composed of the EC states' central bank governors, in addition to five renowned monetary-policy experts, including Jacques Delors. In 1989, the committee drafted the Delors Report,[44] a blueprint for European monetary union. Due to the nature of the committee's composition—experts holding similar monetary-policy beliefs—and its considerable political clout, Verdun (1999a) has characterized it as an actual "epistemic community."

The Delors Report, like the earlier Werner Plan, proposed a three-stage approach to achieve EMU. It also identified the ESCB's prime purpose to be price stability. The June 1989 European Council meeting endorsed the Delors Report. In addition, it was then agreed to convene two intergovernmental conferences (IGCs), in December 1990, with the aim of reaching agreements on both EMU and on European Political Union (EPU).[45]

For several years, the EMS had appeared to be a rather stable construct. In the first years of its existence, several realignments had occurred, involving many EMS currencies. Pressures to appreciate were extensive for the German mark and for the Dutch guilder (and since 1983 also for the Belgian and Luxembourg francs). By comparison, the French franc, Italian lira, and Irish punt were devalued several times during the course of the 1980s. In the late 1980s and early 1990s, however, realignments of the central rates were rare, leading several observers to assume that the EMS had significantly contributed to sustainable long-term exchange-rate stability among EC member states.

As inflation rates decreased in EC states, there also appeared to be a convincing trend toward convergence. A time-series of inflation rates illustrates the convergence. In Table 2.3, figures are shown from 1979, the year in which the EMS was established, until 1995.

Whereas in 1980, for example, the (nonweighted) average inflation rate was 14 percent for the twelve states that were EC members as of 1986, average inflation rates for this group decreased to 6.5 percent by 1990. A further significant reduction in inflation rates in the early 1990s was likely reinforced by the formulation of the TEU convergence criteria. The average of inflation rates in 1995 was only 3.4 percent, with a similarly low standard deviation among these rates of 2.3. Generally, however, the trend to lower inflation applied to both ERM and non-ERM countries (including the United Kingdom during the course of the 1980s).

For some EC states, the overall reduction in inflation rates was quite impressive. Greece, for example, had an inflation rate of almost 25 percent in 1980, Italy of 21.2 percent, and Ireland and the United Kingdom of 18.2 and 18 percent, respectively. By 1990, the highest inflation rates among the EC states were 20.4 percent for Greece and 13.4 percent for Portugal. By 1995, however, these rates had decreased

Table 2.3 A Time-Series of Inflation Rates[a] for the EC-12, EMS 1979–1995

	1979	1980	1981	1982	1983	1984	1985	1986	1987	1988	1989	1990	1991	1992	1993	1994	1995
Belgium	4.5	6.6	7.6	8.2	7.7	6.3	4.9	1.3	1.6	1.2	3.1	3.4	3.2	2.4	2.8	2.4	1.5
Denmark	9.6	12.3	11.7	10.1	6.9	6.3	4.7	3.6	4.0	4.6	4.8	2.7	2.4	2.1	1.3	2.0	2.1
France	10.8	13.6	13.4	11.8	9.6	7.4	5.8	2.7	3.1	2.7	3.6	3.4	3.2	2.4	2.1	1.7	1.8
Germany	4.1	5.5	6.3	5.3	3.3	2.4	2.2	-0.1	0.2	1.3	2.8	2.7	3.6	4.0	3.6	2.7	1.8
Greece	19.0	24.9	24.5	21.0	20.2	18.4	19.3	23.0	16.4	13.5	13.7	20.4	19.5	15.9	14.5	10.9	9.3
Ireland	13.3	18.2	20.4	17.1	10.5	8.6	5.5	3.8	3.1	2.1	4.1	3.3	3.1	3.1	1.4	2.3	2.6
Italy	14.8	21.2	17.8	16.6	14.6	10.8	9.2	5.8	4.7	5.1	6.3	6.5	6.3	5.2	4.5	4.0	5.2
Luxembourg	4.5	6.3	8.1	9.4	8.7	5.6	4.1	0.3	-0.1	1.4	3.4	3.7	3.1	3.2	3.6	2.2	1.9
Netherlands	4.2	8.5	6.7	5.9	2.7	3.3	2.3	0.1	-0.7	0.7	1.1	2.5	3.9	3.2	2.6	2.8	1.9
Portugal	23.9	16.6	20.0	22.4	25.5	28.8	19.6	11.8	9.4	9.7	12.6	13.4	10.9	9.0	6.4	4.7	4.1
Spain	15.6	15.6	14.5	14.4	12.2	11.3	8.8	8.8	5.2	4.8	6.8	6.7	6.0	5.9	4.6	5.2	4.7
United Kingdom	13.4	18.0	11.9	8.6	4.6	5.0	6.1	3.4	4.1	4.9	7.8	9.5	5.9	3.7	1.6	2.5	3.4
Average EC-12	11.5	14.0	13.6	12.6	10.5	9.5	7.7	5.4	4.3	4.3	5.9	6.5	5.9	5.0	5.3	3.6	3.4
Standard deviation	6.4	6.3	6.0	5.7	6.8	7.4	5.9	6.6	4.7	3.8	3.9	5.5	4.9	3.9	4.9	2.6	2.3

Sources: Qvigstad (1992) for figures 1979 to 1990; *Eurostat* for figures 1991–1995; own calculations.
Note: [a]Annual percentage change of the Consumer Price Index (CPI).

to 9.3 percent and 4.1 percent, respectively. By comparison, some EMS member states had relatively stable price levels between 1979 and 1995 (e.g., Belgium, Germany, Luxembourg, and the Netherlands). An impressive gradual lowering of inflation rates can also be seen for Denmark, Spain, France, and Ireland.

A trend similar to that of inflation performance was observed in long-term interest rates (usually measured as interest on government bonds). Between 1979 and the early 1990s a decrease in average long-term interest rates was paralleled by a narrowing of the dispersion among these rates for all EC states.[46]

The reduction of inflation rates, however, was a process not restricted to Europe. Significant changes in inflation performance also occurred for other world actors, including Japan. From 1980 to 1990, as compared to the previous decade, Japan achieved a significant reduction in both its price-level increases and the variability of inflation rates. Starting from a relatively low level, Switzerland also reduced inflation rates between 1980 and 1990 as compared to 1970 to 1980. In the United States, average inflation rates were lower between 1980 and 1990 than in the decade before, although with a somewhat larger variability (an increase of the standard deviation from 2.8 to 3.3 percent).[47]

Indeed, the EMS appeared to be very stable in the late 1980s. Too stable, perhaps, as some prominent economists argued.[48] According to these authors, the stability of the EMS was overdrawn in the sense that realignments that should have taken place failed to occur. Caused not least by the introduction of EMU's stage I on July 1, 1990—leading to the abolition of remaining capital controls—and reinforced by the Bundesbank's policy choice of high interest rates to fight inflationary pressures after German reunification, financial speculation put several EMS currencies under pressure. The removal of capital controls complicated the operation of the EMS.[49]

In September 1992, the Finnish markka, experiencing extensive speculative pressures, was forced to abandon its peg to the ECU and started to float freely. Speculative pressures were also directed against other currencies. The United Kingdom saw itself forced to withdraw the pound sterling from the ERM later that month. Then the central rate of the Spanish peseta was devalued by 5 percent, and the Italian lira temporarily withdrew from the ERM. Shortly thereafter, Italian authorities announced that the lira would be kept outside the ERM until further notice. In November 1992, the Swedish central bank announced the abandonment of the ECU peg and the free floating of the Swedish krona.

On December 10, the Norwegian krona abandoned the ECU peg. In January 1993, after a reduction of British interest rates, the central parity of the Irish punt in the ERM was devalued by 10 percent. The next few months were relatively quiet, but in May 1993 the central rates of the Spanish peseta and of the Portuguese escudo were devalued by 8 and 6.5 percent, respectively. In August 1993, the ministers in the Ecofin Council, together with the central bank governors, agreed to widen the fluctuation bands of the ERM from plus or minus 2.25 percent to plus or minus 15 percent. (Germany and the Netherlands, however, agreed to leave the DM/guilder band unchanged at plus or minus 2.25 percent.)

Negotiations on the creation of a true monetary union, and a single currency for the EU, were largely determined by the relative success of economic integration within the internal market program and the stability the EMS had created for the conduct of monetary policy in Europe from 1979 until the early 1990s, before EMS turbulence set in.

The decision to establish EMU grew from a conviction that EMU could strengthen the internal market and from political attempts to further unify Europe. In theoretical work on convergence and subsequent negotiations on EMU institutionalization, two major schools of thought can be discerned. One argues that distributional concerns were central to the negotiation outcomes on EU monetary integration, whereas the other one emphasizes that learning was important. Walsh (2000) labels these contrasting explanations the "distributional bargaining approach" and the "learning explanation," respectively. According to this categorization, prominent work in the "distributional bargaining approach" includes De Grauwe (1993), Garrett (1994), Grieco (1995), Moravcsik (1998), and Oatley (1997). Crucial contributions to the "learning explanation," by comparison, are Sandholtz (1993); Cameron (1995); Dyson, Featherstone, and Michalopoulos (1995); McNamara (1998); and Verdun (2000). The debate over which approach better explains the causes of convergence of macroeconomic and monetary policies in Europe, however, is not yet settled. Walsh, on the basis of his own empirical analysis, attributes more weight to arguments based on the distributional bargaining approach. He suggests that Germany was one of the most influential bargaining powers and bases this suggestion on the reasoning that outcomes most closely reflect the preferences of the states least interested in reaching agreement.[50]

The EMS was a precursor to EMU, but the transition from the EMS to EMU did not happen according to the pure logic of market forces. Rather, it reflected preference convergence, a desire to reap economic gains through integrated monetary policies and to firmly anchoring a larger Germany in the EU construct. It also reflected a general political momentum for even deeper integration in Europe.

Notes

1. Goddard (2003: 241); Spero and Hart (2003: 14).
2. Russia, which participated in the negotiations at Bretton Woods, was unable to stay within the system and participate in its new institutions, mainly because its conception of what constituted desirable patterns of global economic and monetary governance differed from that of Western countries.
3. Spero and Hart (2003: 14).
4. Goddard (2003: 242).
5. Heisenberg (1999: 22).
6. Ibid. (16).
7. Ibid.
8. Spero and Hart (2003: 17).
9. Ibid.
10. Triffin (1960).
11. Spero and Hart (2003: 17).
12. Ibid. (24).
13. On the "dollar crisis," see Strange (1972).
14. Eichengreen (1996: 137).
15. Babarinde (2003: 311).
16. Babarinde (2003: 295), Eichengreen (1996). For a detailed analysis of the Snake, see Tsoukalis (1977).
17. Eichengreen (1996: 156).
18. Ibid. (155).
19. Ibid. (154).
20. Gros and Thygesen (1998: 17); Eichengreen (1996: 156).
21. Eichengreen (1996: 155).
22. Spero and Hart (2003: 25).
23. Tsoukalis (1977); Jones (2002: 6). Also see Heisenberg (1999: 25–26).
24. McNamara (1999: 456).
25. Eichengreen (1996: 159).
26. See Heisenberg (1999: 18).
27. Bernhard and Leblang (2002: 804-805).
28. De Grauwe (1989).
29. Sandholtz (1993); McNamara (1998).
30. Heisenberg (1999: 4).
31. Eichengreen (1996: 160).
32. Heisenberg 1999: 21. On relations between the Bundesbank and the German government, also see Kennedy (1991), Goodman (1992), or Loedel (1999).
33. Jones (2002: 7).
34. A detailed account of the negotiations on the EMS is given in Ludlow (1982). For a description of the early history of the EMS, see Gros and Thygesen (1998).

35. Babarinde (2003: 296).

36. The ECU, then called the European Unit of Account (EUA)—which also constituted a basket of EC members' currencies—was used in the 1970s in the framework of the European Development Fund and the European Investment Bank and as a unit of account for the EC budget.

37. Babarinde (2003: 311). However, the ECU basket encompassed more currencies than SDRs did. As of January 1999, for example, only four currencies were in the SDR basket: the US dollar (45 percent), the euro (29 percent), the yen (15 percent), and the pound sterling (11 percent). See Goddard (2003: 250).

38. This is a principle that also applies to other currency baskets, including the value of SDRs.

39. Percentage shares of domestic currencies in the ECU basket can be calculated on the basis of the amount of a domestic currency in the basket in relation to its ERM central rate. The central rate of the German mark to the ECU, for example, was 1.91 (i.e., 1.91 marks to one ECU). In order to calculate the percentage share of the German mark in the ECU basket, the fixed amount of German marks in the basket (0.6242) can be divided by the ERM central rate (1.91) in order to obtain the percentage share of the German mark in the ECU basket (32.68 percent, or 0.6242/1.91 = 0.3268). When the German mark appreciated vis-à-vis the ECU, the German mark central rate was decreased (i.e., more ECUs were obtained for German marks).

40. "The currency composition of the ECU basket shall not be changed." See Article 109g of the TEU.

41. See Kennedy (1991), Loedel (1999).

42. Babarinde (2003: 296).

43. European Commission (1990).

44. Committee for the Study of Economic and Monetary Union (1989).

45. Babarinde (2003: 297).

46. For respective figures, for example, see Qvigstad (1992).

47. Tavlas (1993: 568).

48. See Eichengreen and Wyplosz (1993).

49. Eichengreen (1996: 139).

50. Walsh (2000: 154).

3

Toward the Creation of European Economic and Monetary Union

In discussions about monetary integration in Europe, a central debate divided actors. At issue was whether European monetary union should be achieved first, allowing domestic economies to gradually adjust in response to the new circumstances (according to the "monetarist approach"), or member state economies should converge first and a unified currency be established in the sense of a crowning achievement to economic convergence (according to the "economist approach"). Heisenberg (1999: 25–26) describes the divisions within the EU on the preferred process to reach EMU: The European Commission and government delegates of France, Belgium, and Luxembourg favored an approach by which EC member states' exchange rates would be locked early in an effort to create the discipline necessary for macroeconomic convergence. According to this monetarist approach, EC member states would need to adjust their domestic economic policies in an effort to prepare for the new single currency, since the option of devaluation would no longer be feasible within a monetary union. By comparison, actors favoring the economist approach, represented notably by the governments of Germany and the Netherlands, argued that monetary union would only be feasible after a phase in which countries still had the option of adapting the exchange rate of their domestic currency. Merging currencies without first ensuring economic convergence could risk fracturing EMU.

The debate over these different approaches toward monetary union is reflected, to a certain extent, in the TEU provisions regarding EMU. These provisions set clear dates for the transition to monetary union, while unequivocally requiring prior convergence in economic and fiscal terms.

Another issue that surfaced during discussions over monetary union was the question of symmetry. In institutional terms, the creation of an EMU on the basis of symmetric influence (in the framework of a new kind of "EuroFed") was favored by member states that had little de facto leverage within the EMS. For example, a more symmetric institutional foundation appears to have been crucial to France, including the French central bank and the ministry of finance.[1] The provisions in the TEU and its protocols on decisionmaking, as well as the overall institutional structure of EMU, reflect this desire for more symmetry. Accordingly, EMU is constituted as a system in which all participating members hold equal influence (irrespective of factors such as population size or economic weight). The European System of Central Banks (ESCB), which is composed of the ECB and the national central banks, is governed by the ECB's governing council. The governing council comprises the members of the ECB's executive board and the governors of the national central banks. The members of the executive board have eight-year terms in office, and, to shield the members from political pressure, the terms are nonrenewable. In moving toward EMU, national central banks, moreover, had to become fully independent, a requirement designed to further protect EMU from possible political pressures.

Historical experience, however, may qualify the importance of formal symmetry. Both the Bretton Woods system and the EMS were designed as symmetric institutional structures, but both evolved into highly asymmetric regimes in practice.[2] The US dollar developed into the effective anchor in the framework of the Bretton Woods fixed exchange-rate regime, and the German mark clearly assumed this role in the framework of the EMS. Because EMU is more institutionalized than either Bretton Woods or the EMS were, however, this formal symmetry may be more realistic in the framework of the ESCB, resulting in EMU resembling the US Federal Reserve System rather than the EMS in this sense. Considerably larger EMU membership in the future would likely enhance this tendency.

In contrast to EMU, in structural terms the EMS was based on the principle of voluntary membership, since members could leave the ERM when their currency experienced severe pressures (although such action, of course, could have repercussions on domestic economic policies as well as the credibility of domestic monetary institutions). Nonetheless, exchange-rate adjustments were generally possible, since the EMS—like the Bretton Woods system, according to its institutional rules—constituted a system of fixed but adjustable rates. In a sense, the

EMS was a multispeed approach to European integration, because only some of the EC member states—although a majority—participated in the ERM. However, all currencies of EC member states formally participated in the EMS (notably in the ECU currency basket).

The TEU was signed in February 1992 and entered into force on November 1, 1993. This treaty constituted the legal basis for EMU and its new single currency. On the basis of high-level expert advice, notably the 1989 Delors Report, the treaty stipulated that the creation of EMU would be accomplished in three stages. In addition, it spelled out the conditions for member states' participation in the final stage of EMU.

Stage I, effective July 1, 1990, implemented—as part of the internal market program—free movement of capital within the EC, aimed to reinforce economic convergence among EC member states, and instituted an evaluation by the Ecofin Council of progress achieved toward convergence.

Stage II, to become effective January 1, 1994, would entail the establishment of the EMI, the preparation of full independence of national central banks, a prohibition of monetary financing of the budget by central banks, the monitoring of the budgetary situations of EU states, and the coordination of macroeconomic policies.

Stage III, to be implemented January 1, 1999, at the latest, was to constitute the effective start of EMU with the introduction of one common currency, establishment of the ECB, and an effective changeover to the euro in the financial markets of all participating member states.

At the European Council meeting in Madrid on December 15 and 16, 1995, participants decided to name the new single currency the euro and confirmed the starting date for the third stage as January 1, 1999.

The TEU and the attached protocols described the factors that were to be crucial in decisions about which members would qualify to enter EMU from its inception and whether EMU would start with a majority of the EU states. The price-stability entry criterion stated that, in the twelve months prior to evaluation, a member's inflation rate should not exceed by more than 1.5 percentage points that of "at most" the three best performers. Assessed at the beginning of 1992, for example, this relative figure would have been an inflation rate of 4.4 percent (see Table 2.3 on p. 29).[3] Assessed in 1988, however, this relative criterion would have been 1.3 percent, and at the beginning of 1995, the benchmark would have been an inflation rate of 3.5 percent. Although these criteria appeared to be somewhat arbitrary from an economic point of view, they provided clear targets for domestic monetary policies and

were flexible in the sense of allowing assessments of relative performances of EC states rather than absolute performances. By comparison,
fiscal targets were more fixed and not defined in relative terms.

In the twelve months preceding examination for EMU participation,
according to the provisions of the TEU, long-term interest rates (usually
interest rates on government bonds) were not to exceed by more than
two percentage points the (nonweighted) average of the long-term interest rates of the three best inflation performers. Since the three best inflation performers in 1991 were Denmark, Ireland, and Luxembourg, for
example, and the (nonweighted) average of their long-term interest rates
was 9.6 percent, the relative benchmark on interest rates for 1992 would
have been 11.6 percent.

The criterion regarding exchange-rate stability was somewhat difficult to interpret in practice. According to the criterion, a country's
exchange rate was to have remained, in the two years prior to the examination date, within the "normal fluctuation margins" of the ERM.[4]
However, when these convergence criteria were defined, the normal
fluctuation margins within the EMS were still plus or minus 2.25 percent, but the margins had been widened to plus or minus 15 percent in
the aftermath of the 1993 currency turmoil. Hence, the interpretation of
this criterion and of what constituted normal fluctuation margins was
essentially up to political judgment.

Two important criteria referred to EU states' fiscal performance.
The first held that the ratio of the general government deficit to GDP
could not exceed 3 percent. The second prescribed that government debt
as a share of GDP had to be equal to or less than 60 percent (or should
at least clearly be moving toward this target).

Hence, the monetary variables were defined in relative rather than
absolute terms, and there was no indication of maximums regarding
inflation or interest rates. The two fiscal criteria were more fixed and
particularly important because the EMS had led to some convergence
regarding inflation and reduced exchange-rate variability, although it
had not really induced fiscal convergence (which can be decisive for the
conduct of monetary policy). Table 3.1 summarizes the convergence criteria as stipulated in the TEU.

To judge the capacity of different EU members to join EMU
according to these criteria, Table 3.2 provides an overview of the performance of the fifteen EU states as of 1996 with respect to inflation,
interest rates, government deficits, and government debts. However, it
does not refer to the requirement regarding exchange-rate stability due
to the less straightforward interpretation of this criterion after the
widening of ERM bilateral fluctuation margins in 1993.

**Table 3.1 Convergence Criteria Qualifying EU States for EMU
Membership**

Criteria	
Inflation	Not exceeding 1.5 percent plus average of (at most) the three best performers of the twelve months before the examination date.
Interest rates	Not exceeding 2 percent plus average of (at most) the three best performers in terms of inflation rates of the twelve months before the examination date.
Exchange-rate stability	Remained within the normal fluctuation bands of the ERM in the two years before examination date.
Budget deficit	General government deficit to be less than, or equal to, 3 percent of GDP.
Government debt	To be less than, or equal to, 60 percent of GDP (or to approximate this target).

As Table 3.2 illustrates, the average yearly inflation rate of the fifteen EU states was 2.6 percent, indicating a decrease as compared to earlier rates (see Table 2.3). Moreover, the new EU members as of 1995—Austria, Finland, and Sweden—fit well into this overall trend. Similarly, the relative dispersion of price-level changes among the fifteen EU states was again lower than before (see Table 2.3), with a standard deviation of 1.9. The figures given in Table 3.2 demonstrate that the EU states, in the mid-1990s, had converged to a considerable extent regarding price stability. Indeed, the standard deviation (in percentage points) of nonweighted annual average inflation rates decreased from 5.5 percent at the end of 1990 to about 1.9 percent in 1996 and decreased again in the following years, reaching less than 1 percent in the beginning of 2004.[5]

However, some states faced difficulties meeting the criterion regarding price-level increases. For example, Greece—despite an impressive lowering of its inflation rate as compared to earlier periods of its EMS membership—still experienced a relatively high annual inflation rate. Italy, Portugal, and Spain, although having inflation rates above the EU average, had managed to significantly moderate their domestic price-level increases (possibly in an effort to belong to EMU's core group).

EMS members with weaker currencies also tended to have higher long-term interest rates. Most affected by this phenomenon were Greece, Italy, Portugal, and Spain. However, long-term interest rates were also

Table 3.2 Performance of the EU-15 Regarding Four Convergence Criteria, in 1996

	Inflation rates	Long-term interest rates (in percent)	General government surplus or deficit (in percent of GDP)	General government debt (in percent of GDP)
Austria	1.7	6.5	−4.3	71.7
Belgium	1.6	6.7	−3.3	130.6
Denmark	2.2	7.4	−1.4	70.2
Finland	0.9	7.4	−3.3	61.3
France	2.1	6.6	−4.0	56.4
Germany	1.3	6.3	−4.0	60.8
Greece	8.4	15.1	−7.9	110.6
Ireland	2.1	7.5	−1.6	74.7
Italy	4.7	10.3	−6.6	123.4
Luxembourg	1.3	7.0	−0.9	7.8
Netherlands	1.2	6.3	−2.6	78.7
Portugal	3.0	9.4	−4.0	71.1
Spain	3.8	9.5	−4.4	67.8
Sweden	1.6	8.5	−3.9	78.1
United Kingdom	3.0	8.0	−4.6	56.3
Average	2.6	8.2	−3.8	74.6
Standard deviation	1.9	2.2	1.8	28.8

Source: European Monetary Institute (1996: iv).

somewhat elevated for other EU members, including Ireland, Sweden, and the United Kingdom.

It is not necessarily the case that larger membership automatically implies more leverage in international financial relations. Factors such as price stability and fiscal discipline were viewed to be more important in determining EMU's potential importance in global monetary relations than the mere number of members. If convergence criteria were interpreted loosely, leading to an early acceptance of EC states with weak economic and monetary fundamentals, EMU's role in the world economy would likely be weakened rather than strengthened. Consequently, several powerful actors within the EU, including the government of Germany, advocated a strict maintenance of fiscal and monetary criteria in order to ensure EMU stability in the long run. Accordingly, the difficult road toward convergence in monetary and fiscal policies induced some of the core members of the EMS, notably Germany, to also press for application of stringent criteria once EMU had started, to avoid negative repercussions of "free-riding effects," such as excessive domestic government spending and ensuing inflationary pressures, which might cause euro-area interest rates to rise.

The SGP, agreed upon in June 1997, gave clear compliance benchmarks regarding fiscal policy. It was, in turn, criticized for these rigorous targets and a lack of flexibility, especially its inability to account for differences in member states' business cycles.[6]

In comparison with later developments, the years in which the convergence criteria were formulated suggested positive prospects for enhanced fiscal discipline for several EC member states. Germany, for example, had a government deficit of 2.7 percent of GDP in 1990 and a ratio of government debt to GDP of 44.5 percent. Other EC member states achieved similarly satisfactory fiscal balances.[7] Moving toward monetary union appeared to be very feasible on the basis of fiscal indicators. These fiscal balances reinforced optimistic evaluations of long-term trends toward low budget deficits and decreasing debt ratios and supported movement toward EMU in the short-term future. Simultaneously, they strengthened actors supporting the initiation of the SGP.

In 1996, government deficits among EU states were highest in Greece and Italy. The largest figures on government debt—resulting from a series of budget deficits in the course of the 1980s—existed in Belgium, Greece, and Italy (Table 3.2). However, economic downturn, starting in the early 1990s, forced several EU member states to increase government spending, for unemployment benefits for example. Simultaneously, tax receipts dropped. Hence, budget deficits worsened rather than improved, similarly aggravating the debt to GDP ratio for many EU states. In Germany, the budget was put under additional strains by high public expenditures related to German reunification. In order to cover the new financial needs, largely those in the formerly eastern parts of Germany, and to fight inflation, German interest rates were kept elevated. This forced other EMS members to keep their domestic rates high, in order to defend ERM parities, despite an urgent need to stimulate domestic demand by reducing interest rates. These elevated rates, in addition to the full abolition of capital controls in 1990, enhanced speculative capital movements and largely induced the 1992–1993 exchange-rate turbulence.

Germany partially failed to comply with the fiscal convergence criteria in the mid-1990s: For example, Germany's budget deficit for 1995 was 3.3 percent of GDP.[8] In 1996, it again exceeded the 3-percent target. Although Germany had been one of the driving forces behind the

definition of the convergence criteria, and later the SGP, fearing inflationary bias within EMU if respective fiscal aims were not incorporated
into a pact, it was, along with France, one of the large EU countries that
found fulfilling the SGP criteria difficult. This trend increased in the
first years of EMU.

In the late 1980s and early 1990s, meeting the convergence criteria
as stipulated in the TEU had seemed feasible in practice. However, economic downturn changed the situation. Several EU states had difficulties coping with various aspects of the convergence criteria, notably
those relating to fiscal targets. In view of members' difficulties with fulfilling the criteria as laid down in the TEU, there was considerable
debate on EMU postponement. As the European economies gradually
moved out of economic recession, however, adherence to the overall
EMU timetable seemed increasingly likely. Moreover, the fact that
interpretation of the convergence criteria offered some room to maneu-
ver decreased the possibility that the criteria themselves would have to
be weakened formally.[9] With the application of various flexible accounting methods, all fifteen EU states—both "Euro-11" and "non-Euro 11"
states (i.e., EU states that started with EMU on January 1, 1999, and EU
states remaining outside)—formally met the convergence criteria regarding budget deficits in 1998. Table 3.3 gives an overview of budget
deficits or surpluses for 1998. There appeared to be no formal obstacles
regarding this conversion criterion.

The official decision on which EU states complied with the convergence criteria and whether a majority of EU members fulfilled them
was to be made by the European Council in 1997. The basis for the
decision was to be a report by the European Commission and a recommendation by the Ecofin Council (on the basis of a qualified majority
vote of EU member states). Hence, political institutions were going to
assess member states' economic performance and compliance with the
convergence criteria.

But was the time for the establishment of EMU ripe? Economists
strongly disagreed on this question. Clearly, public opinion in EU states
did not always favor the envisioned, somewhat quick, transition to EMU.
Table 3.4 indicates that, according to opinion polls, EMU did not have
all that much backing among EU citizens at the end of 1997. However,
public opinion changed rapidly, and before the actual start of EMU a
clear majority of EU citizens expressed themselves as being in favor of
monetary union. Governmental campaigns aiming to increase public
awareness of, and support for, EMU may indeed have achieved the

Table 3.3 Budget Deficits/Surpluses of EU States as Percentage of GDP, 1998

EU States	Budget Deficit (–) or Surplus (+)
Euro-11 States	
Austria	–2.2
Belgium	–1.5
Finland	+0.8
France	–2.9
Germany	–2.4
Ireland	+2.5
Italy	–2.6
Luxembourg	+1.4
Netherlands	–1.2
Portugal	–2.3
Spain	–1.9
Non-Euro-11 States	
Denmark	+1.0
Greece	–2.7
Sweden	+1.2
United Kingdom	–0.4

Source: The *Economist,* January 2, 1999.

desired results. The percentage of citizens favoring EMU broadly increased in the years before the actual start of monetary union.

Table 3.4 shows the percentage of citizens in individual EU states who expressed themselves as in favor of EMU at the end of 1997 and in mid-1998.[10] Significant increases in the percentage of citizens supporting monetary union can especially be seen for Austria, Finland, Germany, Luxembourg, and the Netherlands. Support for EMU seemed to be quite extensive from the beginning, and stable, in Italy and Ireland.[11]

Public opinion in Britain, Denmark, and Sweden remained consistently among the most skeptical regarding monetary union.[12] Opinion-poll data also indicated, however, that fairly large percentages of the European population did not feel well informed about EMU. In 1995, only 20 percent of the people polled in Eurobarometer studies indicated that they felt well informed about the new currency. By 1998, this share had increased to 34 percent.[13] Hence, the share of citizens feeling informed about EMU, as well as the percentage of those expressing themselves in favor of the euro, increased as the start of EMU approached.

Table 3.4 Percentage of EU Citizens Expressing Themselves as in Favor of EMU, end of 1997 as compared to mid-1998

Euro-11 Member States	Percentage in Favor of EMU	
	End 1997	Mid-1998
Austria	44	56
Belgium	57	68
France	58	68
Finland	33	53
Germany	40	51
Ireland	67	68
Italy	78	83
Luxembourg	62	79
Netherlands	57	73
Portugal	45	52
Spain	61	72
Average Euro-11	54.7	65.7
Standard deviation	13.1	11.2

Source: The Economist, January 2, 1999, based on *Eurobarometer* and *Keesing's* data; own calculations.

Among the factors influencing support rates for the euro and monetary policy delegation to the ECB appear to be national identities, domestic economic performance, and general support for the EU.[14] In the first years of EMU, average support for the euro remained stable at approximately 70 percent for the then twelve participating countries.[15]

On December 31, 1998, acting on a proposal of the European Commission and after consultation with the ECB, the European Council adopted the euro's "irrevocable conversion rates."[16] These rates became effective for all EMU member states at 0.00 on January 1, 1999 (local time). Because of the sequence of local time zones, Finland was the first EU state to formally join EMU. The new conversion rates were to be the only ones EMU states would use for exchanges between the euro and national currency units, as well as for conversion between domestic currencies. Table 3.5 provides an overview of the euro's irrevocable rates for the eleven EU states that entered EMU on July 1, 1999.

The fixed euro conversion rate for the Greek drachma, entering EMU in 2001, was 340.750 Greek drachmas per euro. Six digits were given for the conversion rates in order to allow for precision in respective exchanges. The new conversion rates replaced market and central

Table 3.5 Euro Conversion Rates, effective 0.00 January 1, 1999 (local time)

Domestic Currency	Value of one euro expressed in units of the domestic currency
Austrian schilling	13.7603
Belgian franc	40.3399
Dutch guilder	2.20371
Finnish markka	5.94573
French franc	6.55957
German mark	1.95583
Irish pound	0.787564
Italian lira	1936.27
Luxembourg franc	40.3399
Portuguese escudo	200.482
Spanish peseta	166.386

Source: ECB.

rates as used within the EMS. The announcement of the conversion rates, therefore, allowed economic agents and consumers all over the EU to anticipate the value of domestic currencies in euros without remaining margins of uncertainty.

According to the schedule for the implementation of EMU, euro notes and coins became legal tender on January 1, 2002. On the same day, EMU states started issuing euro notes and coins. Denominations for the coins are one, two, five, ten, twenty, and fifty cents, as well as one and two euros. The new euro coins were designed to combine a preservation of national symbols with the introduction of new, European ones. One side of the euro coins displays symbols common to all EU member states, whereas the other side is characterized by explicitly national symbols. For example, Germany uses an oak twig on its one-, two-, and five-cent coins, and the Brandenburg Gate on its ten-, twenty-, and fifty-cent coins. In addition, the federal eagle is used on one- and two-euro coins. These symbols were already familiar to the German public from the coins used in the era of the German mark.

In technical terms, the introduction of the euro was a smooth endeavor. On January 1, 2002, more than 80 percent of automated teller machines in the euro area were dispensing euros.[17] By the beginning of January 2002, about 6.5 billion euro notes, worth about 134 billion euros, had been distributed, mainly to central banks and credit institutions inside and outside the euro area.[18] Similarly, almost 38 billion coins, with a total value of 12.4 billion euros, were disseminated in this way.

The introduction of the euro, in technical terms, was what may be viewed as a masterpiece. By July 2002, domestic currencies in the euro area were withdrawn. Although criticism regarding the feasibility and desirability of EMU still existed, with the successful introduction of the euro, the ECB's clear emphasis on price stability and independence from political pressure, and the smooth technical transition to EMU, the strength of critical voices gradually decreased.

Notes

1. See Dyson and Featherstone (1996).
2. McKinnon (1993).
3. The figure is calculated by taking the inflation performance of the three best performers in 1991—Denmark, Ireland, and Luxembourg, summing up their rates (2.4 + 3.1 + 3.1), dividing by 3, and adding 1.5 percent to this (non-weighted) average.
4. See Article 109j of the TEU: "the observance of the normal fluctuation margins provided for by the exchange-rate mechanism of the European Monetary System, for at least two years, without devaluing against the currency of any other Member State."
5. For respective information, based on ECB data, see Aziz (2004: 35).
6. See Begg (2002). See also, Chapter 5 in this book.
7. For exact figures, e.g., see Qvigstad (1992).
8. Data from *Eurostat*.
9. See Leblond (2003).
10. For percentage shares for 1995 through 1998, based on *Eurobarometer* data, broken down by EU states, see Weishaupt (2003: 7–8).
11. Among the six original EC member states, Italy has consistently had strongest domestic support rates for the euro. See Banducci et al. (2003: 691).
12. Banducci, et al. (2003: 691).
13. Weishaupt (2003: 7).
14. Kaltenthaler and Anderson (2001).
15. See Babarinde (2003: 310), based on data from Eurobarometer 55 (October 2001).
16. The announcement of these rates occurred in May 1998.
17. Babarinde (2003: 308).
18. Ibid.

4

The Structure of the European Central Bank System

On June 1, 1998, the ECB was established in Frankfurt am Main, Germany. The ESCB comprises the ECB and the national central banks of all EU states (fifteen members until May 2004 and twenty-five since then).[1] The Eurosystem encompasses the ECB and the national central banks of EU states participating in EMU. EU states not in the Eurosystem are ESCB members with a special status. With EU enlargement to twenty-five members, the number of representatives in the ESCB has grown significantly. The new EU member states as of May 1, 2004, are Cyprus, the Czech Republic, Estonia, Hungary, Latvia, Lithuania, Malta, Poland, Slovakia, and Slovenia.

The ECB is governed by an executive board and by a governing council. The conduct of monetary policy for the euro area is the responsibility of the ECB's governing council. The implementation of EMU monetary- and exchange-rate policies by national central banks is mainly supervised by the ECB's executive board.

The ECB executive board comprises the ECB president and vice-president and four other members. Generally, executive board members are presumed to defend a "euro-area perspective" within EMU. They are appointed by unanimous consent of the European Council.[2] Table 4.1 shows the composition of the ECB executive board as of January 2005.

Among the major tasks of the ECB executive board are the implementation of monetary policy according to the guidelines provided by the governing council and the formulation of respective instructions to national central banks. Procedurally, the executive board often acts as an agenda setter, presenting the governing council with proposals to be discussed and then either accepted or rejected.[3] The executive board

47

Table 4.1 Composition of the ECB Executive Board, January 2005

President	Jean-Claude Trichet (since November 1, 2003)
Vice-President	Lucas D. Papademos (since June 1, 2002)
Member	José Manuel González-Páramo
Member	Gertrude Tumpel-Gugerell
Member	Otmar Issing
Member	Tommaso Padoa-Schioppa

conducts informal and often bilateral discussions with national central bank presidents.

The ECB governing council comprises the six members of the ECB's executive board and the central-bank presidents of the Eurosystem states. Among the main tasks of the ECB's governing council is the formulation of monetary policy for the euro area, which includes decisions on key interest rates, promotion of a smooth operation of payment systems, and the managing of official reserves of the members of the Eurosystem. The composition of the ECB governing council is shown in Table 4.2. The president of the Ecofin Council and a member of the European Commission may participate in the meetings of the governing council, but they hold no voting rights.[4]

Formally, the governors of national central banks hold equal voting power within the ECB governing council on the basis of one country, one vote. The European Commission, during the preparations for the IGC on monetary union in 1990, had proposed a weighted voting scheme for the governing council. But the proposal faced opposition, not least by the Bundesbank and the German ministry of finance, partially due to fears that national interests would promote a spirit of bargaining and compromise instead of a focus on general euro-area interests.[5]

Governing council decisions, according to the ECB's statutes, are made on the basis of simple majority rule. In practice, decisions are usually reached by consensus. However, the current voting system will become impractical with considerable EMU enlargement. Reducing the size of the governing council therefore appears to be central to the maintenance of decisionmaking efficiency in this institution.[6] Possibilities for reform include the introduction of rotating representation in the governing council,[7] grouping of member states by geographical areas, or

Table 4.2 Composition of the ECB Governing Council, January 2005

President	Jean-Claude Trichet
Vice-President	Lucas D. Papademos
Member of the ECB Executive Board	José Manuel González-Páramo
Member of the ECB Executive Board	Gertrude Tumpel-Gugerell
Member of the ECB Executive Board	Otmar Issing
Member of the ECB Executive Board	Tommaso Padoa-Schioppa
Governors (Presidents) of the National Central Banks:	
Klaus Liebscher	Austria
Guy Quaden	Belgium
Axel A. Weber	Germany
Nicholas C. Garganas	Greece
Erkki Liikanen	Finland
Christian Noyer	France
John Hurley	Ireland
Antonio Fazio	Italy
Yves Mersch	Luxembourg
Nout Wellink	Netherlands
Vítor Manuel Ribeiro Constâncio	Portugal
Jaime Caruana	Spain

delegation to experts.[8] The governing council, indeed, put forward an official proposal based on a rotation system, as it viewed such a system as most representative of euro-area interests and as avoiding many of the pitfalls of alternative voting systems. However this proposal has been criticized, not least by the European Parliament (EP), partially because the new voting system appears quite complex. The EP and the European Commission, moreover, favored a more thorough reform of the ECB's governance structures in view of enlargement.

As not all EU states belong to the Eurosystem, an ECB general council is also in operation. The general council comprises the president and vice-president of the ECB and the governors of the EU national central banks. The remaining executive board members may participate in meetings of the general council, but they do not have the right to vote.[9] In essence, the general council has taken over the responsibilities of the former EMI. Among the general council's most important current tasks are the collection of statistical information, the preparation of annual ECB reports, and the establishment of rules to standardize accounting and operations reports of national central banks for EU states both within and outside the Eurosystem.

Jean-Claude Trichet and Lucas Papademos—and before them Willem Duisenberg and Christian Noyer—are members of the general council, as are the representatives of all EU national central banks. The general council also includes three central bank governors not members of the governing council, namely the central bank governors from EU states not currently in the Eurosystem. In 2004, these members were Bodil Nyboe Andersen (governor of the central bank of Denmark), Lars Heikensten (governor of the Swedish central bank), and Mervyn King (governor of the Bank of England).

The governors of the central banks of all new EU states since May 2004 are now members of the ECB's general council. They will, however, not join the governing council until they adopt the euro. The addition of ten states to the governing council in the medium-term future, possibly to be followed by at least two others shortly thereafter (Bulgaria and Romania), makes stalemate on monetary policy within the governing council a likely scenario. One potential conflict concerns systematic differences in monetary-policy preferences between small, fast-growing states, notably those located in Central and Eastern Europe, and slower-growing, low-inflation countries.[10]

The institutions of the Eurosystem are supposed to be fully independent of political pressures, and provisions were implemented to increase the likelihood that the ECB is indeed fully independent in practice. For example, governors of national central banks, as well as members of the ECB executive board, have long-term contracts. For central bank governors, the term in office is minimally five years, and these terms are renewable. For ECB executive board members, the term in office is a minimum of eight years, although these terms are nonrenewable.[11] Nonetheless, voting records are not available for governing council meetings, and the possibility that central bank presidents at times give priority to the concerns of their own country rather than those of the euro area cannot be excluded. The fear of such distortions is prominent in discussions on institutional representation in the governing council, not least because smaller states are reluctant to abandon their vote in the council due to fears of domination by larger states.[12]

Measures to ensure independence of the ECB, however, are anchored institutionally. Leblond (2004: 38) mentions various important elements: The ECB and the ESCB may not "seek or take" instructions from any EU body or member-state government; the ECB has the exclusive right to issue bank notes within EMU; the ECB and national central banks are prohibited from extending any form of credit to EU institutions, member-state governments at any level, or any other public authorities; any measures to provide privileged access for EU bodies or member states' governments to financial institutions, or to other public authorities, are prohibited; the EU and the member states are not liable for debts incurred by other member states; all national central banks within the Eurosystem have to be legally independent; and finally, the ECB is managed by the governing council, consisting of the governors of national central banks and the ECB's executive board.

Because the economies in the euro area are diverse and business cycles do not usually coincide, much research has focused on how to allow for a coherent, efficient monetary policy for the euro area.[13] One of the most significant problems for EMU is that, due to different domestic monetary transmission mechanisms, EMU states have different preferences when it comes to decisions to increase or decrease euro-area interest rates and different assessments of the magnitude of effects such changes in interest rates may generate domestically.[14] Effects of interest-rate changes are different, for example, depending on structures of EU states' household debt patterns.

The irrevocable fixing of exchange rates within the euro area has deprived economic agents of the macroeconomic tool of adjusting exchange rates to enhance the international competitiveness of their export industries. For example, in the early stages of the EMS, France adopted a policy to increase economic growth rates and reduce unemployment while accepting relatively high inflation levels, which brought on consecutive devaluations of the French franc. Such a policy is no longer feasible within EMU. Clearly, EMU has constrained domestic macroeconomic policy options for EMU member states.

The ESCB's unequivocal task is defined as maintenance of price stability.[15] The distribution of competencies between the Ecofin Council and the ECB, notably with regard to exchange-rate policy, has been a matter of discussion during the negotiations on EMU, since this strongly determines the extent to which the ECB can, in fact, be independent. The distribution of policy functions, according to the provisions of the TEU, is as follows: the Ecofin Council is responsible for the conclusion of formal monetary agreements, and the ECB is responsible for the management of reserves and the implementation of EMU day-to-day exchange-rate policy. The Ecofin Council's decisions need to be unanimous and are made on the basis of recommendations of the European Commission or the ECB.

For example, formal international exchange-rate arrangements involving the euro need to be unanimously decided in the Ecofin Council.[16] According to provisions of the new EU draft constitution, measures relating to the euro's role in the global monetary system in a broad sense would need to be decided by a vote of those EU states in the Ecofin Council that are part of the euro area. For example, Article III-90 of the draft constitution stipulates: "In order to secure the euro's place in the international monetary system, the Council of Ministers, on a proposal from the Commission and after consulting the European Central Bank, shall adopt a European decision establishing common positions on matters of particular interest for economic and monetary union within the competent international financial institutions and conferences." For (qualified) majority decisions regarding international monetary policy and coordination, only representatives in the Council of Ministers participating in the euro area hold voting rights.[17] Consensus among these same members in the Council of Ministers is required for unanimous decisions. Hence, the constitution establishes a kind of "Ecofin Council for the euro area," according to a proposal made earlier by the European Commission. In 1997, a Eurogroup was established as an informal forum for discussion between the finance ministers of euro-area states. However, with the EU draft constitution, decisions were to be allocated to the Ecofin Council, notably its subgroup of euro-area finance ministers. Accordingly, every EMU member state, irrespective of its fiscal or economic performance, holds a veto right regarding decisions for which unanimity among the euro-area finance ministers is required. This veto power will be extended to future EMU members.

The difficulty of reaching unanimity in an enlarged EMU, however, is likely to reduce prospects for formal international exchange-rate arrangements involving EMU.[18] A model like the Bretton Woods system therefore would be unlikely for the future. "General orientations for exchange-rate policy" in relation to "one or more non-Community currencies" (TEU Article 109.2) could, however, be formulated on the basis of a qualified majority vote in the Ecofin Council (with other relevant institutions having consultative power on this). Similarly, Article III-83 of the EU draft constitution stipulates: "In the absence of an exchange-rate system in relation to one or more third-country currencies . . . , the Council, acting by a qualified majority on a recommendation from the Commission after consulting the European Central Bank, may formulate general orientations for exchange-rate policy in relation to these currencies." Clearly, informal monetary agreements will be easier to conclude for euro-area states.

An earlier example of such a pattern of informal multilateral cooperation is the 1985 Plaza Agreement. In September 1985, finance ministers and central bank governors of the G-5 states held a secret meeting at New York City's Plaza Hotel, where they essentially agreed to lower the external value of the US dollar (after a phase of significant dollar appreciation from 1983 through 1985).[19] A similar arrangement was reached in the 1987 Louvre Accord, in that case in an attempt to stem the dollar's depreciation.[20]

EU enlargement in May 2004 by ten new member states, and the likely admission of several new states into EMU in the medium-term future, may make both informal and formal exchange-rate arrangements even more difficult to achieve.

The Ecofin Council, on the basis of TEU Article 109.1, had a large say regarding the adaptation, adjustment, and, finally, abandonment of the central rates of the EMS regime. TEU provisions also provided for some Ecofin Council influence regarding the euro's exchange rate, although this influence was clearly constrained by the ECB's mandate to maintain price stability. Geoffrey Garrett (1994) points to the fact that the respective provisions of the TEU (mainly Articles 105, 109.1, and 109.2) partially contradicted each other regarding which institution (the ECB or the Ecofin Council) would in practice determine exchange-rate policy in EMU. This ambiguity likely reflects dissent among EC member states in the intergovernmental negotiations on EMU. Whether this partial ambiguity will influence ECB policy in the future remains to be seen.

How could this distribution of responsibilities affect the orientation of exchange-rate policy in the euro area more generally? Is a conflict of interest possible within the ECB regarding price stability and an (active) exchange-rate policy? A stable external value of the euro might benefit its potential international use. The primacy of price stability is likely, however, to limit the ECB's options and willingness to actively influence the euro exchange rate vis-à-vis third currencies. An example from earlier experiences within the EMS may illustrate this situation.

In the aftermath of German reunification, the Bundesbank's tight monetary policy aimed to counteract potential domestic inflationary pressures. These pressures, in part, stemmed from the terms on which

German monetary union had been achieved, not the least of which was the comparatively favorable exchange rate granted to the former East German currency. The Bundesbank's main focus on price stability forced it to maintain high interest rates, whereas Germany's EMS partners, faced with economic recession, urgently needed a lowering of Germany interest rates. While a domestic focus on price stability is acknowledged by a majority of central bankers to provide a sound basis for long-term economic performance[21] and enhance prospects for international use of the currency, this prioritization may prevent central bankers from engaging in international activities aimed at maintaining exchange-rate stability.

At the same time, the German government believed that the mark's exchange rate was crucial in this case due to the importance of exports for the German economy. Thus, it viewed a stable exchange rate facing little upward pressure as beneficial for the economy. With this view, it may have had priorities partially contradicting those of the Bundesbank.

Similarly, the level of trade openness of European economies, which differs significantly from the lower level of trade openness of Japan or the United States, for example, may cause tensions between those EMU governments desiring a stable and rather low level of the euro and the general objectives of the ECB.[22]

Generally, countries with a longer tradition of political influence channels to central banks may be inclined to try to carry exchange-rate policy partially into the ECB (although the statutory rules for the ESCB clearly counter such endeavors). In fact, Article 2 of the TEU required the ECB to support the EU's ultimate objectives of full employment, growth, and equitable income distribution, although this requirement is hardly emphasized by the ECB.[23]

Enlargement of EMU might, if preferences for an active ECB growth-oriented policy exist in new member states, affect the ECB's future attitude regarding the trade-off between maintenance of price stability and an active exchange-rate policy. In the years since its creation, however, the ECB has demonstrated clear reluctance to take an active stance regarding the euro's external value, at least as long as depreciation would not—via higher import prices—imply a risk of inflationary pressure.[24] The orientation of the ECB toward its price-stability mandate in the context of the euro exchange rate has been demonstrated in various editorials, speeches, and public comments of representatives of the ECB governing council.[25]

Another issue, finally, has raised much discussion regarding the institutional structure of EMU. Is democratic legitimacy compatible with full ECB independence? Is the ECB possibly too remote from political discussions and oversight? Arend Lijphart (1999) argues that it is failure by political executives to grant more independent power to central banks that weaken democratic systems. Accordingly, democratic practice may be most elaborate when price stability is the major, or only, objective in the central bank's charter and the central bank holds the final word in cases of conflict with other government objectives.[26] Similarly, an independent ECB can lead to more stability within political systems when potentially divisive discussions on monetary policy are delegated to an independent central bank rather than fought out within government coalitions.[27]

Critics have claimed that the democratic foundations of the ECB are questionable and that its institutional design lacks democratic accountability and responsiveness.[28] In general terms, there may be a certain trade-off between democratic legitimacy and effective decisionmaking, and this trade-off may also refer to patterns of voting in the ECB.[29] Increasing output efficiency, in the sense of monetary-policy outcomes strengthening legitimacy in the long run, is defended by some authors (e.g., Issing 1999). Similarly, "legitimacy through results," advocated by the ECB itself, argues that more transparency in the governing council's decisionmaking process would not benefit the legitimacy of the institution, because it is, for the most part, policy outcomes that should be relevant to the public. Critical voices still hold, however, that accountability and democratic legitimacy are insufficient and that the EP in particular needs to obtain a more prominent role in ECB accountability.

Discussions on the ECB's "democratic deficit" are certainly not closed yet. It remains to be seen how they will develop after significant future EMU enlargement. In general terms, the EU draft constitution has not changed the TEU's provisions regarding ECB accountability.

Notes

1. For a detailed overview of the structure of the ESCB and the ECB, see Loedel (2002).
2. See Levitt and Lord (2000: 204).
3. Heisenberg (2003: 407).
4. Leblond (2004: 38).
5. Dyson and Featherstone (1999: 383); see Heisenberg (2003: 403).
6. See Baldwin et al. (2001a,b).
7. This suggestion has been endorsed by the ECB: "at the December 2000 Nice summit, the Member States agreed to hold a special intergovernmental conference to deal just with central bank reform. As a result, in December 2002, the ECB proposed reforming the voting in the Governing Council by

establishing three classes of rotation, with larger GDP countries voting more often than smaller countries. . . . This proposal was unanimously adopted by the ECB Governing Council." Heisenberg (2003: 405).

8. Experts in the sense of "apolitical technocrats." This suggestion has been made most prominently by Baldwin et al. (2001b).

9. See Article 45.2 of the Statutes of the ESCB and of the ECB.

10. Heisenberg (2003: 400).

11. Some members have shorter tenure, however, to allow for continuity regarding the subsequent composition of the executive board.

12. Heisenberg (2003: 411).

13. See de Grauwe (2000).

14. See de Grauwe (2000).

15. See Article 2, Chapter II of the TEU: "In accordance with article 105(1) of this Treaty, the primary objective of the ESCB shall be to maintain price stability. Without prejudice to the objective of price stability, it shall support the general economic policies in the Community with a view to contributing to the achievement of the objectives of the Community as laid down in Article 2 of this Treaty. The ESCB shall act in accordance with the principle of an open market economy with free competition, favouring an efficient allocation of resources, and in compliance with the principles set out in Article 3a of this Treaty."

16. The first part of Article 109 in the TEU described the procedure—then still for the ECU—in detail: "By way of derogation from Article 228, the Council may, acting unanimously on a recommendation from the ECB or from the Commission, and after consulting the ECB in an endeavor to reach a consensus consistent with the objective of price stability, after consulting the European Parliament, in accordance with the procedure in paragraph 3 for determining the arrangements, conclude formal agreements on an exchange-rate system for the ECU in relation to non-Community currencies."

17. A qualified majority for such decisions is defined to be a majority of the votes of the representatives of EU states in the euro area, with this majority representing at least three fifths of the total euro area population.

18. Also see Henning (1994) and Kahler (1995).

19. Eichengreen (1996: 147–149).

20. See Spero and Hart (2003: 38–39).

21. Kaltenthaler (2003: 335).

22. On preferences of EMU central bankers regarding the euro's exchange rate, see Kaltenthaler (2003). On preferences of economic actors regarding the level and relative stability of exchange rates, see Frieden (1991).

23. Beber (2003: 77). The EU draft constitution (Article 29), similarly, has a provision that the ECB, "without prejudice to the objective of price stability, . . . shall support general economic policies in the Union with a view to contributing to the achievement of the Union's objectives."

24. Kaltenthaler (2003).

25. A passage from a speech by Willem Duisenberg from March 1999 characterizes this policy stance: "The primary objective of the single monetary policy is the maintenance of price stability. Monetary policy will always be geared to this objective. Consequently, the monetary policy strategy of the Eurosystem

does not embody an implicit or explicit exchange rate target or objective, since gearing monetary policy decisions to maintaining such an exchange rate target may, at times, conflict with the goal of price stability." Quoted in Kaltenthaler (2003: 339).

26. Lijphart (1999: 232); Aziz (2004: 4).

27. Bernhard and Leblang (2002).

28. For voices critical of the ECB's democratic deficit, see Elgie (2002), Verdun and Christiansen (2001), Dyson and Featherstone (1999), Dyson (2002), Berman and McNamara (1999), Buiter (1999), Hodson and Maher (2002). Less critical regarding the ECB's potential lack of democratic accountability are, for example, Heisenberg and Richmond (2002) and Crombez (2003). For a respective overview of arguments regarding the existence of an EMU democratic deficit, see Aziz (2004).

29. Heisenberg (2003: 398).

5

Exchange Rates, Monetary Policy,
and Fiscal Stability

In a technical sense, the transition to the euro in 2002 was almost flaw-less[1]: no upheavals whatsoever in existing monetary and banking systems in the EU occurred. This success is especially amazing considering the difficulties related to the introduction of the new common currency[2]: millions of prices had to be adapted, cash-dispensing machines, parking meters, and vending machines had to be redesigned, and a multitude of databases had to be converted.[3]

In spite of the successful introduction of the euro, however, the new European currency started its existence in a somewhat troubled way. In the first year after its formal introduction on January 1, 1999, the euro lost considerable value compared, for example, to the US dollar. By the end of 1999, the value of the currency had dropped by about 10 percent.[4] As an average over 2001, the euro was exchanged at 0.89 US dollars.[5] But is it bad for a currency to lose relative external value? Certainly, the fact that the euro's exchange rate dropped to such an extent may have added to economic and political actors' perception that the currency—and the monetary policy guiding it—was not fully credible. A currency's relative strength is just one aspect of its overall role, however. A low external value of a currency benefits specific economic interests. In general, a domestic currency's low exchange rate provides a competitive advantage for exporters, as their goods become less expensive on international markets. On the other hand, however, the weakness of the euro could affect the potential strength of the EU economy by making raw materials, including oil (which is usually priced in dollars), more expensive to import.[6]

As mentioned previously, the ECB was reluctant to support the external value of the euro. Only if the euro's exchange rate held a risk of inflationary pressures for the euro area did the institution appear to be concerned. In turn, the US administration of George W. Bush was pressured to ease its own strong dollar policy—a policy somewhat inherited from the Clinton administration—because it made US products more expensive abroad. There was a risk that demand for US products could decline, with negative repercussions for the already serious US trade deficit.

Internationally coordinated attempts to strengthen the external value of the euro, however, were rather scarce. A common effort of the United States, Japan, and the ECB during a G-7 meeting in September 2000 managed to increase the euro exchange rate from approximately eighty-six to ninety euro cents per US dollar. However, after the somewhat shaky start in terms of the euro's external value—but not in terms of the ECB's clear commitment to price stability—the value of the euro gradually increased. On average over 2002, it was exchanged at 0.95 US dollars and at 1.13 US dollars on average over 2003.[7]

The euro's apparent weakness in global exchange markets in the first year of its existence resulted in criticism of the ECB and its first president, Willem Duisenberg. In addition, considering the fact that Europe was threatened by the possibility of economic downturn, it was unclear why the ECB was reluctant to cut interest rates in the interest of stimulating European economies. Why was the ECB so slow reacting to market pressures, especially as compared to the US Federal Reserve, an institution pursuing an active domestic monetary policy and at times operating like a motor for global monetary and financial affairs? Why did the ECB not act as swiftly and smoothly in order to allow market participants to regain trust in the strength of the economy and in the ECB's guidance in macroeconomic and monetary policies? Why could Duisenberg's activities not be compared to the demonstrated skills of an Alan Greenspan?

While some of the criticism raised against the ECB's policies may have looked convincing at first, one important fact does have to be kept in mind: the ECB was not designed as a political institution that would operate to smooth circumstances in real markets. The one overarching goal of the ECB, indeed, is maintenance of price stability (which is also understood to be the best tool for long-term economic growth). The ECB's independence from politics, and strict orientation toward price stability, led many US observers to criticize this young institution and its leadership and brought some European criticism of the ECB's policies. Why did the ECB not pursue more active growth-oriented policies that would help European economies recover and, especially, alleviate the major problem of comparatively high unemployment rates that plagued several EU states? The seriousness of this problem is illustrated in Table 5.1, which gives an overview of unemployment rates across Europe in 2002 and 2003. Average unemployment among the twenty-five EU states was about 8.5 percent in both years, with a fairly high, although decreasing, standard deviation among these rates. Some of the new EU states, in particular, were facing high unemployment rates. The 2003 unemployment rate in Poland was 19.2 percent; in the Slovak

Table 5.1 Unemployment Rates of the EU Member States, 2002 and 2003

EU Member States	Unemployment Rate	
	2002	2003
Austria	4.2	4.3
Belgium	7.3	7.9
Cyprus	*3.9*	*4.5*
Czech Republic	*7.3*	*7.8*
Denmark	8.7	9.6
Estonia	*11.3*	*11.3*
Finland	9.1	9.0
France	8.9	9.5
Germany	8.7	9.6
Greece	10.3	9.7
Hungary	*5.6*	*5.7*
Ireland	4.3	4.6
Italy	9.0	8.6
Latvia	*12.5*	*10.4*
Lithuania	*13.6*	*12.7*
Luxembourg	2.8	3.7
Malta	*7.7*	*8.0*
Netherlands	2.7	3.8
Poland	*19.8*	*19.2*
Portugal	5.0	6.2
Slovak Republic	*18.7*	*17.5*
Slovenia	*6.1*	*6.5*
Spain	11.3	11.3
Sweden	4.9	5.6
United Kingdom	5.1	5.0
Average	8.4	8.5
Standard deviation	4.4	3.9

Source: Data from European Central Bank (2005: 40); own calculations.
Note: New EU states as of 2004 presented in italics.

Republic, it was 17.5 percent. By comparison, unemployment rates were fairly low in Austria, Luxembourg, and the Netherlands. However, with unemployment rates in 2003 of 9.6 percent and 9.5 percent respectively, both France and Germany, were facing pressures to their existing patterns of macroeconomic governance and the constraints imposed by fiscal coordination within the EU, including the SGP.

Unemployment rates across Europe, as compared to rates in other advanced industrialized democracies, tend to be fairly high. Table 5.2 provides respective figures for the EU-15, Japan, and the United States from 1993 through 2004. Although the average unemployment rate in the fifteen EU states tended to decrease after 1995 and in the beginning of the new millennium, it was still a few percentage points above rates prevailing in the United States and Japan.

Different traditions within Europe regarding the desired role of a central bank appeared to clash: some EU governments favored a central bank actively promoting economic policies that could especially dampen unemployment, whereas others expected the institution to concentrate on price-level stability exclusively, according to the ECB's mandate as defined in its statutes.

Generally, the ECB's clearly defined goal of price stability prevents it from conducting any growth-oriented policies. Still, some authors appear to favor an independent institution that nonetheless facilitates some macroeconomic growth and policy convergence in the euro area.[8] According to others, including Issing (1999) and Alesina et al. (2001), however, it is price stability exclusively that ensures economic growth in the long run. A short-term growth-oriented strategy of the ECB, according to these authors, can only be counterproductive in the medium- to long-term future.

International political economy literature has highlighted the fact that, in general, interest group behavior concerning exchange rates is not very pronounced. It is possible to distinguish between domestic groups favoring either stable or more flexible exchange rates and those favoring a high level versus a low level of the external value of the domestic currency (Frieden 1991). However, since it is difficult to understand how monetary policies affect the real economy and what would be the consequences of different monetary policy options, there is a significant lack of agreement about what constitutes good macroeconomic policy.[9] Also somewhat unclear are the distributional effects of monetary policies. In contrast to interest group activity in other economic areas, notably trade policy, uncertainty about the effects of monetary policy on the real economy appears to translate into inaction on the part

Table 5.2 Unemployment Rates[a] of the EU-15, the United States, and Japan, 1993–2004

Year	1993	1994	1995	1996	1997	1998	1999	2000	2001	2002	2003	2004
EU-15	10.1	10.5	10.1	10.2	10.0	9.4	8.7	7.8	7.4	7.7	8.1	8.0
United States	6.8	6.1	5.6	5.4	4.9	4.5	4.2	4.0	4.8	5.8	6.0	5.5
Japan	2.5	2.9	3.1	3.4	3.4	4.1	4.7	4.7	5.0	5.4	5.3	4.8

Source: Eurostat
Notes: [a]Unemployed persons as a percentage of total labor force.

of domestic interest groups and reduce sectoral and firm activity aiming at influencing the level of the exchange rate.[10] In Europe, domestic policymakers are not usually subject to extensive lobbying on monetary or exchange-rate issues. The same holds true for the ECB. Generally, low lobbying activity regarding monetary policy tends to be supported by relative institutional insulation of treasury and central bank officials from societal pressures.[11]

Interestingly, with the rise in the external value of the euro, critics of the ECB's policies seemed to become less vocal. After all, the euro seemed to be a strong currency in global monetary affairs. But is this relation between the external value of a currency and popular perception of the adequacy of central bank policies justified? Indeed, a currency tends to appreciate if demand for it is high, making it "strong" in a more common sense, but one does have to keep in mind that the external value of a domestic currency always creates winners and losers domestically: some domestic groups (notably income-competing industries) will favor a relatively elevated exchange rate, whereas others clearly favor a low external value of the domestic currency.[12] As mentioned previously, export sectors generally tend to benefit from, and therefore favor, a low external value of the domestic currency. Nonetheless, such preferences are rarely articulated politically.

There are trade-offs regarding the conduct of monetary policy and the possibility of autonomous economic policy making, as described by Robert Mundell's "assignment problem."[13] According to Mundell's proposition, only two of the following can hold simultaneously: a fixed exchange rate, free capital flows, and monetary policy autonomy. Hence, in a world of mobile capital, when a government aims to keep its exchange rate fixed—as within the EMS—national monetary policies must focus on maintaining exchange-rate stability and cannot be directed toward other goals.[14] Similarly, with capital mobility and fixed exchange rates—as within EMU—domestic monetary policy choices are severely limited.

However, with capital mobility and fixed exchange rates, fiscal policies can be relatively more flexible. European states appear for the most part to follow domestic rationales in the management of their fiscal policies.[15] Indeed, a striking asymmetry characterizes patterns of macroeconomic and fiscal governance in the EU: whereas in most political systems, including many federations, responsibility for overall fiscal policy, taxation, and macroeconomic policy is at the central government level, the EU lacks significant powers in these policy domains.[16] Moreover, matters related to EU-level fiscal policy and taxation need to be decided unanimously by EU governments. This provision was even maintained in the EU's draft constitutional treaty, drawn up by the European Convention during the course of 2002 and 2003. Along with other sensitive policy areas, including Common Foreign and Security Policy (CFSP), the common decision procedure in the field of fiscal policy is unanimity.

The Open Method of Coordination (OMC), the principles of which were introduced in the TEU regarding economic policy (and later applied especially to the question of employment at the Amsterdam IGC), was endorsed at the 2000 Lisbon summit meeting of the EU. In the framework of the OMC, economic, social, and environmental policies aiming at long-term economic growth, but on the basis of social sustainability, are pursued. The OMC also induces EU states to coordinate their macroeconomic policies on an essentially voluntary basis, although this clearly does not lead to a unified macroeconomic approach in the EU. Indeed, increasingly, cooperation in macroeconomic policies occurs through the soft instruments characterized by the OMC.[17] Within the euro area, therefore, macroeconomic policy is not truly coordinated. There are several initiatives to get the economies of EU member states into tune, for example through the tool of the Broad Economic Policy Guidelines (BEPG), formulated by the European Commission. BEPGs, presenting both general and country-specific macroeconomic recommendations, outline medium-term economic policy strategies for the EU that are consistent with the Lisbon strategy. They aim in particular at stability-oriented macroeconomic policies and socially sustainable economic reform policies. But there are no true fiscal and macroeconomic competencies at the central EU policy level, even for just the Eurosystem states. Instead competencies in the area of macroeconomic policy, including those presented in the framework of the OMC, appear to constitute a patchwork, in which coordinated approaches are still lacking.

Critics of EMU would argue that it might, in this situation, have been better not to initiate EMU: the project, according to this perspective, simply appears to be premature. In the medium to long run, EMU, due to nonharmonized domestic economies, might lead to disagreement and conflict within the euro area and possibly within the EU itself, with detrimental effects on prospects for prosperity, welfare, and harmony among states.[18] On the other hand, the activities and achievements of the ECB, considering the novelty of the EMU project and the challenges the ECB faces in view of the disparity of macroeconomic conditions and needs within its member states, appear impressive. After all, price stability is clearly being maintained, with an attempt to keep yearly inflation at or below 2 percent, and the euro is gaining the image of a young, but strong, and reliable world currency.

The discussion on Optimum Currency Areas (OCAs)[19] and the application of these theoretical approaches to the EU indicates that the euro area may indeed not be flexible regarding labor mobility and wages in particular. Of even more concern to some EMU critics is the fact that business cycles in EMU states are not harmonized.[20] Economic shocks in one part of the monetary union might negatively affect the entire euro area. The monetary and, especially, fiscal convergence criteria defined by the TEU, as well as the provisions of the SGP, were to ensure that EMU would be sustainable in the long run without too much upheaval within the system. However, the economic usefulness of both the TEU criteria and the provisions of the SGP have been challenged.[21]

In contrast to some other political systems, the EU essentially lacks authority to conduct coordinated macroeconomic policies. Given that the ECB sets interest rates centrally for the euro area, there is a striking absence of policymaking in the macroeconomic policy sphere that could parallel efforts in the monetary realm.

Responsibility for trade policy, for example, traditionally rests with the central EU institutions (formerly those of the EC). After all, the creation of a Customs Union (CU), as envisioned for the EC in the late 1950s, shifted authority to set tariffs and rates for customs duties from the domain of domestic politics to the supranational level.[22] Whereas in the framework of a Free Trade Agreement (FTA), member states retain power to set tariffs but need provisions (such as rules of origin) to avoid imports through the country with the lowest external rate, CUs apply harmonized external tariff rates at the borders with third countries.[23] Similarly, the CAP, set up in the EC with the aim of avoiding food shortages as experienced during and after World War II, is centralized at the supranational level. The various tools used to sustain farmers' incomes under these schemes, including compensating duties, import levies, and price supports, are determined on the central level. Even prices for agricultural products are set on the basis of political agreement by the Ecofin Council.

Hence, the gap between responsibilities of the EU in the areas of trade or agriculture and those in the domains of fiscal policy, taxation, and macroeconomic policymaking appears to be large. This variation in the relative degree of integration is difficult to explain, but the transaction-based theory of integration, for example, aims to explain just such divergence.[24] According to this view, it is the extent of existing transactions in a policy domain that determines the demand of domestic actors—via EU institutions—for more integration.

Without the ability to conduct a common fiscal policy for the euro area, other tools had to be created to avoid "beggar-thy-neighbor" policies and potential fiscal irresponsibility of EMU members, which might generate inflationary pressures for the euro area. Although the TEU established entry criteria, follow-up provisions were not given. In an effort to remedy this situation by political agreement, major EU governments, notably Germany,[25] pressed for a pact that would continue to control the fiscal behavior of governments in the euro area after the start of EMU.

The SGP essentially created an obligation for EMU member states to avoid excessive domestic budget deficits. It established detailed surveillance procedures with recommendations to be taken by the Ecofin Council on possible sanctions. Fiscal stability was reinforced in order to ensure that EMU would be stable and sustainable in the long run.

However, several politicians were confronted with increasing domestic rates of unemployment, which may have been partly induced by the very restructuring generated by the internal market program, and general economic downturn in the early 1990s. The SGP constituted a compromise solution in which guarantees for budget stability were imposed on participating EMU states and political attempts were made to create institutions that would monitor economies and ensure that some political clout was used to defend employment levels. The logic of the latter approach may not always be entirely clear, since, in the medium term, such policies may often result in even more need for restructuring so that they increase unemployment rather than decrease it. But for the purpose of defending EMU in view of public opinion in several skeptical publics of EU states, the strategy certainly did make sense.

The SGP, without doubt, continued some of the pressures EU states had experienced in preparation for the establishment of EMU: whereas the uncertainty surrounding the question of who would be able to join EMU and which criteria would be applied to determine membership did indeed induce an impressive extent of fiscal discipline among prospective EMU member states, the SGP was primarily meant to maintain this pressure also after EMU started.

The way the pact worked was that EU institutions, mainly the Ecofin Council, would monitor the fiscal performance of Eurosystem states. Governments not complying with the given criterion of constraining budget deficits to 3 percent of GDP at the maximum would first receive warnings. Eventually, however, they would have to pay fines. The SGP may have induced some fiscal responsibility, but it was, as is often the case within the EU, largely a product of political decisions. The pact has been criticized on various grounds, not least because the detailed criteria it stipulated appeared not to be based on transparent theoretical foundations.[26]

In practice, maintenance of the agreed ceilings on budget deficits was difficult. Ireland, Portugal, Germany and, later, France did not meet the targets. Ireland and Portugal, after receiving a warning, did cut public expenditures, despite adverse economic conditions, in an attempt to comply with the requirements of the SGP.

Compliance with the SGP criteria, however, induced criticism, not least in one of EMU's core countries: Germany. After all, when economic recession sets in, it is difficult to curtail public expenditures in order to reduce the budget deficit. How can public expenditures be lowered when more people are unemployed, tax receipts decrease, and unemployment and social security expenditures increase? To many, it appears to be awkward to cut public expenditures when the economy goes into recession. Dissatisfaction with the requirements of the SGP was extensive in Germany, but similar opposition could be seen in several other EU states, including France.

The SGP has been criticized mainly on the grounds that, while it provides clear fiscal targets for politicians, it lacks the flexibility needed for economic growth to materialize. A deficit rate of a maximum of 3 percent of GDP for all euro area states appears to be a somewhat arbitrary goal. As Begg (2003) emphasizes, in times of economic downturn, these targets may need to be trespassed. According to the author, it is also likely that new EU states from Central and Eastern Europe will be unable to comply with the SGP budget-deficit criterion once they enter EMU, given that they need to make new investments, for example, for technological innovation and reforms of their social security systems.

A major upheaval to the system, and a clear sign that politics often prevails over economics, was the fact that the SGP was rendered ineffective in the fall of 2003. It was clear that Germany would, two years in a row, be unable to comply with the SGP's provisions regarding the budget-deficit criterion. Similarly, France, in an even somewhat more self-assertive way, signaled its readiness to ignore the SGP's provisions. Several small and medium-sized EU member states, notably the Netherlands, aimed to save the provisions of the pact, fearing the consequences of both a possible loosening of the fiscal criteria within EMU and repercussions if legal provisions could simply be watered down by the EU's larger powers.

Discussions about the rigor with which the provisions of the SGP should be applied also led to disagreement within the Ecofin Council. In essence, the results of these deliberations led to Germany and France being released of their obligations within the SGP, despite the fact that the European Commission took this case to the European Court of Justice (ECJ). It remains to be seen what effects this partial ignoring of common EU provisions will have, not least in view of ongoing processes of adjusting to significant EU enlargement. One somewhat speculative hypothesis is that in an enlarged EU, the political power of larger EU states might prevail more intensively over commonly agreed policies and rules, reinforcing trends of intergovernmentalism over those of supranationalism. In a sense, developments of EU deepening would then be constrained by widening. But other avenues are still conceivable, especially since the ECJ essentially supported the position of the European Commission.

In spite of various hurdles, optimistic accounts would postulate that the general framework of EMU and the ECB are fine: they set general goals for the medium- to long-term future, despite economic challenges, opposition in public opinion, and short-term economic costs. EMU and the ECB are largely products of intergovernmental negotiations; at the time their major elements were agreed upon, no one could foresee the circumstances of the future. It appeared to be quite feasible in the late 1980s and early 1990s to curtail budget deficits and public debts and to stay within the narrow bands of the ERM. Similarly, remaining within the budget limits given by the SGP may have seemed quite realistic in the late 1990s. In both cases, however, market forces and pressures due to deepening economic recession illustrated that the path chosen presented more hurdles than had been anticipated at the time of the respective intergovernmental negotiations. In this sense, unintended consequences materialized.

It is clear that the European economies are still far from acting in concert in macroeconomic terms. The job of the ECB is rather challenging, since it essentially has to react to different circumstances within its area on the basis of harmonized tools—especially setting common interest rates for the euro area. Macroeconomic cooperation among EU states most often occurs on the basis of soft laws. Labor mobility is still not extensive within the EU (as compared, for example, to the United States). Cultural, linguistic, and regulatory and administrative hurdles have only slowly been overcome within the unified market to allow for a gradual increase in the mobility of people, not least academics and professional experts, within the EU. But not every EU country is part of EMU. As a result, there is a pattern of overlapping institutions and responsibilities and of partially interrelated policy competencies.

Despite problems regarding coordination of EU members' macroeconomic policies, as well as challenges in the domain of fiscal policy, it seems that the euro has now become rather stable in practice. In fact, it is gradually developing into a rather strong world currency. But it is clearly difficult for quite a few states in the euro area to maintain the required fiscal targets, especially those regarding budget deficits. However, these developments, in general, do not appear to put the euro under pressure on global markets. Major speculative attacks against the euro have not occurred on financial markets, indicating that international financial actors may not view these problems as significant enough to affect the external value of the euro.

The ten new states that joined the EU in 2004 now participate in the ERM II, a mechanism that keeps their domestic currencies within bands of plus or minus 15 percent from the euro. There are some differences, however, between the old and new EU states regarding rates of both economic growth and inflation. In general terms, economic growth is higher in some new EU states, whereas records regarding inflation performance are more varied. Table 5.3 provides respective figures on economic growth and inflation rates for the EU-25 from 2000 through 2003.

Some new EU member states, including the Czech Republic, Malta, and the Baltic states (Estonia, Latvia, and Lithuania), have impressive records regarding price stability. Inflation rates are also comparatively low in Cyprus. Especially in the Baltic states, low inflation is paralleled by impressive rates of economic growth.

For the twenty-five EU states as of 2004, a trend toward both declining economic growth rates and lower inflation can be discerned: average GDP growth was 4.5 percent in 2000 but decreased to 2.5 percent in 2003, with somewhat increasing variability among these rates. By comparison, average inflation rates for the EU-25 decreased from 3.9 percent in 2000 to 2.5 percent in 2003, accompanied by lower dispersion until 2002. Hence, both the average level of inflation in the EU and the dispersion of these rates among members are fairly low, with the highest inflation rate in 2002 (Slovak Republic) still being below 9 percent. In a comparison with inflation rates experienced by some states within the EMS (see Table 2.3), price-level increases among the EU-25 are quite moderate.

Table 5.3 GDP Growth Rates and Inflation Rates, 2000 to 2003

EU Member States	GDP Growth Rate[a]				Inflation Rate[b]			
	2000	2001	2002	2003	2000	2001	2002	2003
Austria	3.5	0.7	1.4	0.7	2.0	2.3	1.7	1.3
Belgium	3.7	0.8	0.9	1.3	2.7	2.4	1.6	1.5
Cyprus	*5.1*	*4.1*	*2.0*	*2.0*	*4.1*	*2.0*	*2.8*	*4.0*
Czech Republic	*2.9*	*3.2*	*1.5*	*3.7*	*3.9*	*4.7*	*1.4*	*−0.1*
Denmark	2.8	1.4	1.0	0.4	2.7	2.3	2.4	2.0
Estonia	*6.9*	*5.0*	*7.2*	*5.1*	*3.9*	*5.8*	*3.6*	*1.4*
Finland	5.5	0.6	2.3	2.1	3.0	2.7	2.0	1.3
France	3.8	1.8	1.1	0.6	1.8	1.8	1.9	2.2
Germany	2.9	0.6	0.1	−0.1	1.5	2.1	1.3	1.0
Greece	4.2	4.1	3.6	4.5	2.9	3.7	3.9	3.4
Hungary	*5.2*	*3.7*	*3.5*	*3.0*	*9.8*	*9.2*	*5.2*	*4.7*
Ireland	10.0	5.7	6.1	3.7	5.3	4.0	4.7	4.0
Italy	3.1	1.8	0.4	0.3	2.6	2.3	2.6	2.8
Latvia	*6.6*	*7.9*	*6.4*	*7.5*	*2.7*	*2.5*	*2.0*	*2.9*
Lithuania	*3.9*	*5.9*	*6.8*	*9.7*	*1.0*	*1.3*	*0.4*	*−1.1*
Luxembourg	8.9	1.0	2.5	2.9	3.8	2.4	2.1	2.5
Malta	*5.0*	*−0.8*	*2.6*	*−0.3*	*2.4*	*2.2*	*2.6*	*1.9*
Netherlands	3.3	1.3	0.6	−0.9	2.3	5.1	3.9	2.2
Poland	*4.0*	*1.0*	*1.3*	*3.8*	*10.1*	*5.5*	*1.9*	*0.7*
Portugal	3.7	1.6	0.4	−1.2	2.8	4.4	3.7	3.3
Slovak Republic	*2.2*	*3.3*	*4.6*	*4.5*	*12.0*	*7.3*	*3.5*	*8.5*
Slovenia	*4.6*	*3.0*	*3.3*	*2.5*	*8.9*	*8.5*	*7.5*	*5.7*
Spain	4.2	2.7	2.2	2.5	3.5	2.8	3.6	3.1
Sweden	4.4	1.1	2.0	1.5	1.3	2.7	2.0	2.3
United Kingdom	3.1	2.1	1.8	2.2	0.8	1.2	1.3	1.4
Average	4.5	2.5	2.6	2.5	3.9	3.6	2.8	2.5
Standard deviation	1.9	2.0	2.1	2.5	3.0	2.2	1.5	1.9

Sources: Heisenberg (2003: 401-402), European Central Bank (2005: 35–36), own calculations.

Notes: New EU states as of 2004 presented in italics.

[a]Annual percentage volume change of GDP.

[b]Annual percentage change of the HICP.

In terms of public finances, similarly, many of the new EU states as of 2004 are in a relatively favorable situation. Nonetheless, some states clearly surpass the required budget deficit threshold of a maximum of 3 percent of GDP. Table 5.4 shows general government deficits (or surpluses) as a percentage of GDP for 2000 through 2003.

Compared to the performance of EU states in the years before EMU was established, several of the new EU states have sound records of

Table 5.4 General Government Deficits/Surpluses as Percentage of GDP, 2000 to 2003

EU Member States	General Government Deficit (–) or Surplus (+) as a Percentage of GDP			
	2000	2001	2002	2003
Austria	–1.5	0.3	–0.2	–1.1
Belgium	0.2	0.6	0.1	0.4
Cyprus	*–2.4*	*–2.4*	*–4.6*	*–6.4*
Czech Republic	*–3.7*	*–5.9*	*–6.8*	*–12.6*
Denmark	1.7	2.1	0.7	0.3
Estonia	*–0.6*	*0.3*	*1.4*	*3.1*
Finland	7.1	5.2	4.3	2.3
France	–1.4	–1.5	–3.2	–4.1
Germany	1.3	–2.8	–3.7	–3.8
Greece	–4.1	–3.7	–3.7	–4.6
Hungary	*–3.0*	*–4.4*	*–9.2*	*–6.2*
Ireland	4.4	0.9	–0.2	0.1
Italy	–0.6	–2.6	–2.3	–2.4
Latvia	*–2.8*	*–2.1*	*–2.7*	*–1.5*
Lithuania	*–2.5*	*–2.0*	*–1.5*	*–1.9*
Luxembourg	6.0	6.4	2.8	0.8
Malta	–6.2	–6.4	–5.8	–9.6
Netherlands	2.2	–0.1	–1.9	–3.2
Poland	*–0.7*	*–3.8*	*–3.6*	*–3.9*
Portugal	–2.8	–4.4	–2.7	–2.8
Slovak Republic	*–12.3*	*–6.0*	*–5.7*	*–3.7*
Slovenia	*–3.5*	*–2.8*	*–2.4*	*–2.0*
Spain	–0.9	–0.4	–0.1	0.4
Sweden	5.1	2.8	0.0	0.3
UK	3.8	0.7	–1.7	–3.3
Average	–0.7	–1.3	–2.1	–2.6
Standard deviation	4.2	3.3	3.0	3.5

Source: European Central Bank (2005: 41) on the basis of data from the ECB (for euro area) and the European Commission; own calculations.

Note: New EU states as of 2004 presented in italics.

financial stability that are within the boundaries of the earlier Maastricht criteria, as outlined previously. However, some also face significant challenges for the future. Among the new EU states as of 2004, budget deficits are low notably for Latvia, Lithuania, Estonia, and Slovenia. By comparison, high budget deficits can be discerned for the case of the Czech Republic and, somewhat less radically, for the Slovak Republic.

Table 5.5 General Government Debt as Percentage of GDP, 2000 to 2003

EU Member States	2000	2001	2002	2003
Austria	65.8	66.1	65.7	64.5
Belgium	109.1	108.0	105.4	100.0
Cyprus	*61.6*	*64.3*	*67.4*	*70.9*
Czech Republic	*18.2*	*25.3*	*28.8*	*37.8*
Denmark	52.3	49.2	48.8	45.9
Estonia	*4.7*	*4.4*	*5.3*	*5.3*
Finland	44.6	43.8	42.6	45.6
France	56.8	56.5	58.8	63.7
Germany	60.2	59.4	60.9	64.2
Greece	114.0	114.7	112.5	109.9
Hungary	*55.4*	*53.5*	*57.2*	*59.1*
Ireland	38.3	35.9	32.7	32.1
Italy	111.2	110.6	107.9	106.2
Latvia	*12.9*	*14.9*	*14.1*	*14.4*
Lithuania	*23.8*	*22.9*	*22.4*	*21.4*
Luxembourg	5.5	5.5	5.7	5.3
Malta	56.4	62.0	62.3	70.4
Netherlands	55.9	52.9	52.6	54.1
Poland	*36.8*	36.7	41.1	45.4
Portugal	53.3	55.8	58.4	60.3
Slovak Republic	*49.9*	*48.7*	*43.3*	*42.6*
Slovenia	*27.4*	*28.1*	*29.5*	*29.4*
Spain	61.1	57.5	54.4	50.7
Sweden	52.8	54.4	52.6	52.0
UK	42.0	38.8	38.3	39.8
Average	50.8	50.8	50.7	51.6
Standard deviation	29.0	28.7	28.0	27.4

Source: European Central Bank (2005: 42); own calculations.
Note: New EU states as of 2004 presented in italics.

Hungary experienced a hike in its budget deficit in 2002, with a declining trend again thereafter.[27] Budget surpluses, however, were achieved, for example, in Finland, Luxembourg, Ireland, and Sweden. Even in these cases, however, budget surpluses tended to parallel periods of economic recession and decline between 2000 and 2003. Budget positions also worsened for some major EU states, notably France and Germany. Both countries began to exceed budget deficit targets in 2002. After much political deliberation, the provisions of the SGP were loosened in spring 2005.

Regarding the ratio of public debt to GDP, almost all new EU states as of 2004 met the criterion of a maximum debt rate of 60 percent of GDP from 2000 through 2003, indicating a fairly impressive performance in terms of fiscal policies. The average debt rate for the EU-25 increased moderately between 2000 and 2003, but at 51.6 percent it is clearly within the limits of the defined threshold.

For several new EU states, monetary policymaking autonomy was constrained when they pegged their currencies to the euro.[28] The attractiveness of pegging to the euro, and of being a future member of EMU, was determined by the relative success of the euro: a volatile, weak euro can certainly not generate the magnetic effects that a strong, reliable currency does.

Although they are EU members, Denmark, Greece, Sweden, and the United Kingdom were unwilling or unable to join EMU. Greece had difficulties meeting some of the convergence criteria, most importantly the criterion regarding price stability. However, on the basis of an Ecofin decision in June 2000, Greece was admitted into the Eurosystem on January 1, 2001. In the United Kingdom, public opinion showed a clear reluctance to give up the British pound and join EMU. Although Britain's prime minister, Tony Blair, signaled readiness to support joining EMU, the decreasing value of the euro vis-à-vis the British pound rendered support for joining EMU a difficult issue in domestic politics. In fact, support for joining EMU seemed to decrease with the increase in the external value of the British pound as compared to the euro.

While some political and business circles in the United Kingdom may clearly favor adopting the euro, a large segment of the population does not. This is probably the major reason why the Blair government has so far not conducted a referendum on the euro: as much as some government circles might see benefits, especially economic ones, of switching to the euro, it is equally clear to these governmental circles that a referendum would most likely result in a negative outcome.

However, giving up the British pound and exchanging the valued domestic currency with the euro seems inconceivable to many UK citizens. They may also fear being dominated by "the Continent." Maintaining formal sovereignty to conduct one's own monetary policy may seem superior to many, even if, in fact, monetary policy is being strongly conditioned by the policy options chosen for the euro area.

Of course, one might argue that sentiments against the adoption of the euro were also present in other EMU countries, including Germany. After all, many Germans found giving up the cherished German mark very difficult. In several EU countries, the former domestic currency now has the flavor of something cherished from the past.

These backlashes may, in a certain sense, be linked to the generally low support in European publics for EU institutions, as evidenced again, notably in France and in the Netherlands, in the 2005 referenda outcomes on the European Constitution. A similar skepticism may apply to the ECB. After all, these institutions are perceived to be foreign, standing in contradiction to domestic sovereignty and self-rule and not always working to the benefit of one's own country.

Denmark certainly belongs to the more "euroskeptic" EU states. Reluctance to integrate more extensively in security-related domains, for example, was paralleled by a pronounced reluctance to adopt the euro. Similarly, the prospect of joining the euro area was a highly contested domestic political issue in Sweden. In both Denmark and Sweden, public skepticism of EU integration and institutions is pronounced. Neither of these two EU states, however, shares the tradition or experience in international monetary and economic affairs of the United Kingdom—an actor that constituted a global "hegemon" in international financial affairs in the late nineteenth century and the beginning of the twentieth century. In both cases, not only do agricultural interests resent the influence of a perceived Brussels bureaucracy, but people generally fear that EU integration, and notably EMU membership, might profoundly endanger the Scandinavian welfare state. Another Scandinavian country, Norway, remains out even of the EU, after several referenda in the last decades on EC, and later EU, membership were not accepted.

For Denmark and Sweden, as well as the United Kingdom, EMU membership would encroach on domestic sovereignty and the ability to conduct independent social and economic policies. By contrast to Sweden, however, Denmark and the United Kingdom had negotiated an "opt-out" clause regarding EMU in negotiations on the TEU. In Denmark, the TEU was rejected in a domestic referendum in a first round.

Another European country, Switzerland, is now encircled by EU states, and, in fact, by EMU member states. Its policy decisions may be illustrative for other European non-EMU states. A neighbor of Italy, France, Germany, and Austria, this country has similarly gone through a whole series of referenda on EU membership. In each case, the referendum was rejected. This rejection may be partially due to the Swiss institutional requirement of double-majority referenda: when membership in a supranational organization is envisioned, a majority of the population and a majority of the cantons (the Swiss provinces or states) must accept it. These referenda have all caused relatively strong internal political disagreement and cleavages, not least among the different language groups and between cantons located closer to the borders as compared to the center of this small European state. Although the euro can be used along with the traditional Swiss franc in several stores and accounting is often conducted in both currencies, many Swiss citizens, like their counterparts in the United Kingdom, Denmark, or Sweden, can hardly imagine their currency disappearing.[29]

In Switzerland, as in other fairly euroskeptic nations, there are several actors who favor not only EU membership but also membership in EMU. The most prominent argument is that national sovereignty is unfeasible in any case as a consequence of the elaborate trade and economic ties established with the West during the era of the Cold War. Similarly, staying out of the influence of the EU and of EMU is difficult to achieve in an era of regional and global economic interdependence. The largest share of Swiss trade is conducted with its EU neighbors. In addition, EU regulations affect a large part of Swiss domestic rules in just about every area of economic, political, and even cultural life. Considering this reality, is staying out of the EU then an outdated notion? Is it possible de facto to remain sovereign?

Regarding EMU, a moderate extent of monetary sovereignty is possibly feasible in the medium-term future. In the times of the EMS, the Swiss Central Bank, along with EMS members, generally followed the policies of the German Bundesbank. Whereas Swiss monetary policy is not always in correspondence with that of the ECB, it is nonetheless clear that it is strongly influenced by ECB policy. Using the Swiss franc while accepting euros in domestic exchanges may indeed be maintained for several years. In this sense, the Swiss situation appears to resemble the situation in the United Kingdom.

With the establishment of EMU, and the decrease in the euro exchange rate, the Swiss franc, like the British pound, seemed to gain in value. With uncertainties surrounding EMU, capital was moved into both Britain and Switzerland, maybe partly as a diversification strategy of investors aiming to spread currency risk.

For Switzerland, as well as for the current non-EMU but EU member states of Denmark, Sweden, and the United Kingdom, one may assume that tides may change in the future. Pressures of integration crossing borders and affecting so many areas of life, in the medium term, may also affect identities, public opinion, and national sentiments. In this sense, while Switzerland's membership in the EU, let alone in EMU, seems to be unrealistic, and the adoption of the euro by Denmark, Sweden, and the United Kingdom appears to be unfeasible at present, the potential for these states joining EMU in the long run remains. The need for double accounting and continuous calculating on the basis of two currencies complicates business transactions and increases transaction costs for domestic producers and consumers alike. Economic pressures, again, might induce these states—in spite of widespread opposition to the adoption of the new currency—to eventually take the political decision to embark on the road to EMU membership.

Notes

1. See Begg (2003).
2. For an overview of the various challenges to the introduction of the euro, see Flowers and Lee (2002: 10).
3. Babarinde (2003: 304).
4. Collignon and Mundschenk (1999: 1).
5. *ECB Monthly Bulletin,* March 2004, p. 67.
6. On the practice of pricing oil in US dollars and options for the future, see Yarjani (2002).
7. *ECB Monthly Bulletin,* March 2004, p. 67.
8. See Begg (2002); De Grauwe (2003).
9. McNamara (1998, 1999).
10. McNamara (1999: 462).
11. Ibid.
12. See Frieden (1991).
13. The dilemma of policy choices is sometimes referred to as the "unholy trinity." (Mundell 1960; also see Cohen 1977).
14. See McNamara (1999: 458).
15. Garrett (1998); McNamara (1999: 468).
16. See Börzel and Hosli (2003).
17. Begg (2003). On the use of the OMC also see Arnold et al. (2004)
18. See Feldstein (1997a, b).
19. See Mundell (1961), McKinnon (1963), Kenen (1969), Crowley (2002), McKinnon (2004).
20. See Dornbusch (1996).
21. See Buiter et al. (1993).
22. See Viner (1950); Balassa (1961).
23. On the characteristics of FTAs as compared to CUs, see Hosli and Saether (1997).
24. See Stone Sweet and Sandholtz (1998).
25. See Heipertz and Verdun (2004).
26. See Buiter (1999); Leblond (2003), Heipertz and Verdun (2004), Begg (2003).
27. This confirms a trend forecast in Hallet (2004).
28. Heisenberg (2003: 412).
29. After all, it is hard to swallow the factual disappearance of Swissair, another domestic symbol of pride, and the country strongly relies on a culture in which independence, neutrality from large powers, and self-reliance constitute part of national identity.

6

The Euro and the
International Monetary System

W hat will the role of the euro in international affairs be in the future?[1] How significant will this relatively new currency be for both private and public actors? In order to analyze the potential role of the euro in more detail, three main functions of an international currency will be distinguished in this chapter as (1) a unit of account, (2) a means of payment, and (3) a store of value. An overview of these aspects is given in Table 6.1.

The following sections aim to address, on the basis of this categorization, the possible role of the euro in international monetary affairs. The euro's potential significance in the global monetary system is discussed looking at its role as an international *numéraire* (a unit of account), a means of payment, and, finally, as a store of value.

The euro is not the first currency with the potential to constitute a European numéraire. The ECU as a basket currency was established as a European unit of account and created to develop into the EC's official reserve currency. However, in practice, the ECU managed to evolve into neither a significant numéraire nor a common European reserve asset. The official use of the ECU was limited mainly to measuring the size of revolving credits through the European Monetary Compensation Fund (EMCF). However, as a (private) store of value, its role was somewhat more significant, especially regarding ECU-denominated assets (such as ECU commercial paper, notes, and bonds).

The increasing importance of the EU in international trade relations, however, required an adaptation of the formerly modest role of the European currency as a unit of account in international commercial and financial affairs. Since the inception of the EC, the share of intra-community trade as compared to EC members' total share in global

Table 6.1 Functions of International Currencies

Function	Private Use	Official Use
Unit of account	Currency used for foreign trade invoicing, quotation, and denomination of international financial instruments	Currency used in expressing exchange-rate relationships, as an anchor, and for the definition of currency pegs
Means of payment	Currency used to settle international trade, to discharge international financial obligations, and as vehicle currency	Intervention currency in foreign exchange markets, and currency used for balance-of-payments financing
Store of value	Currency in which deposits, loans, and bonds are denominated, and currency used for portfolio allocation	Official reserves and assets held by monetary authorities

Sources: Krugman (1991), Tavlas (1993), Collignon and Mundschenk (1999), Weinrichter (2000).

trade has gradually increased. Early studies suggested, however, that trade creation—the shift from a high-cost domestic production source to a more competitive partner source due to the creation of a customs union—exceeded trade diversion.[2] The developments with respect to the relative shares of intracommunity versus extracommunity trade between 1960 and 1990 clearly demonstrated the trend of increased intraregional exchanges: Assessed for the twelve EC states as of 1986, the percentage share of intra-EC trade was 39.9 percent in 1960, indicating that extracommunity trade clearly exceeded intracommunity trade. By 1975, however, this share had increased to almost one-half of total EC trade (49.5 percent). By 1990, the share of intra-EC trade—again for twelve EC states—surpassed extra-EC trade, with a share in the total of 58.9 percent.[3] However, for the 1990s, a gradually declining reliance on intra-EU trade can be discerned. For the fifteen EU member states as of 1995, shares in intra-EU total imports and exports are shown in Table 6.2 for the time period from 1992 through 2002.

The average shares of intra-EU imports from 1992 to 2002, for the fifteen EU states as of 1995, was 62.2 percent. For exports, this share was 63.2 percent. By comparison, the share of the EU-15 in external trade was comparatively high for Norway and Switzerland, as Table 6.2 illustrates, with Norway having higher export rates to the EU—an average of 76.8

Table 6.2 Trade with the EU-15, 1992 to 2002

Imports[a] (Imp) or Exports[b] (Exp)	EU-15		US		Japan		Canada		Norway		Switzerland	
	Imp	Exp	Imp	Exp	Imp	Exp	Imp	Exp	Imp	Exp	Imp	Exp
1992	64.5	67.0	18.9	24.1	14.5	19.8	10.7	7.4	69.0	78.8	78.5	63.2
1993	62.4	63.2	18.1	21.8	13.7	16.7	9.6	5.9	67.2	78.3	78.8	62.5
1994	62.8	63.3	18.0	21.0	14.1	15.5	9.7	5.4	68.9	77.8	79.2	60.6
1995	64.1	64.0	17.8	21.2	14.5	15.9	10.0	6.4	71.4	77.2	79.8	62.3
1996	63.8	63.1	18.0	20.5	14.1	15.4	10.1	7.0	70.8	76.9	79.0	60.8
1997	62.3	61.8	18.1	20.6	13.3	15.6	9.9	5.2	69.5	76.2	77.1	59.8
1998	63.0	63.2	19.3	22.0	13.9	18.5	9.5	5.1	69.3	77.2	76.8	62.4
1999	62.0	63.8	19.0	21.9	13.8	17.9	10.2	5.6	68.6	73.8	77.8	61.2
2000	59.1	62.4	18.0	21.1	12.3	16.4	10.3	4.6	63.6	76.5	74.5	58.9
2001	59.5	61.9	19.2	21.8	12.8	16.0	11.2	4.5	66.6	76.8	76.2	60.1
2002	60.4	61.8	19.3	20.8	13.0	14.7	11.2	4.4	66.7	75.4	78.0	59.1
Average 1992–2002	62.2	63.2	18.5	21.5	13.6	16.6	10.2	5.6	68.3	76.8	77.8	61.0
Standard deviation 1992–2002	1.8	1.5	0.6	1.0	0.7	1.5	0.6	1.0	2.2	1.4	1.5	1.5

Source: Data from *Eurostat.*
Notes: [a]Percentage of imports from EU-15 of total imports
[b]Percentage of exports to EU-15 of total exports

percent from 1992 to 2002—than import rates (68.3 percent on average from 1992 to 2002) and Switzerland's imports from the EU-15 area exceeding export shares. For Switzerland, average imports from the EU from 1992 through 2002 were 77.8 percent, and exports were 61.0 percent. In both cases, clearly above two-thirds of total trade is with EU neighbors.

For the United States, about one-fifth of total trade is with the EU-15 countries, also with a slightly declining trend for exports in the course of the 1990s. Between 1992 and 2002, the average share of US imports coming from the EU-15 was 18.5 percent, and 21.5 percent of US exports went into this area. Clearly, EU enlargement is likely to increase the EU share in total trade for the United States as well as other countries. From 1992 to 2002, Japan's average imports from the EU area were 13.6 of its total, compared to 16.6 percent of exports. Finally, for Canada, trade with the EU is fairly modest, with imports originating from the EU-15 area averaging 10.2 percent and exports 5.6 percent of its total for 1992 to 2002. In all of these cases, variability in respective trade shares was fairly low, as the standard deviation for these rates from 1992 to 2002 illustrates. Increased intra-EU trade, and higher trade shares of other nations with the EU are likely to materialize due to effects of the considerable May 2004 EU enlargement.

Patterns of trade relations also influence the potential role of a currency in global financial affairs. In the framework of the Bretton Woods system, for example, the United States most likely cared less about the stability of the dollar vis-à-vis other currencies due to its relatively low dependence on international trade. By measuring intra-EU trade as domestic trade, however, the relative international trade-dependence of the EU has also decreased, a trend reinforced by the 2004 enlargement.

In economic terms, increasing shares of intra-EC trade enhanced the need to reduce exchange-rate variability within the EC and necessitated a move toward a system such as the EMS. The aim of reducing exchange-rate volatility within the EC has certainly given a strong impetus to demands for regional monetary integration. Similarly, there was an increasing economic need for a common numéraire, an EC unit of account (a function which the ECU only partially took over in the framework of the EMS, as it was rivaled by EC members' domestic currencies, notably the German mark).

Most EU members have relatively open economies, measured as the ratio of imports plus exports to total GDP. Hence, as compared to other major world actors, such as the United States or Japan, the European economies tended to be more affected by volatility of international exchange rates. Trade openness may also enhance incentives for EMU member states to increase the role of the euro as a unit of account and a means of payment in their trade relations with non-EMU states.

However, the larger the share of intra-EU trade as compared to extra-EU trade, the lower the pressures to aim at external exchange-rate stability. Hence, the contradiction between the priorities of price stability and exchange-rate stability for EMU, as outlined in Chapter 4, may gradually work in favor of the first objective, the larger is the number of EMU members and hence, the percentage share of total intra-EU trade. Clearly, enlargement to 25 EU states, with many of the new member states aiming at future EMU membership, is likely to further enhance this trend.

Generally, given fixed exchange rates within EMU, the larger the share of intra-EU trade, the more incentives for member states to look for different means of economic protection within the EU. The lower the share of extra-EU trade, however, the lower the incentives to search for external arrangements, such as international exchange-rate cooperation, for example.

Regarding the relationship between exchange-rate stability and trade patterns of EMU members, an interesting question is whether eliminating exchange-rate fluctuations in the framework of EMU—and thus completely abolishing member states' macroeconomic instrument of exchange-rate adjustment—might lead to an increase in new forms of protectionism in Europe. Under the EMS regime, some members devalued their national currencies in a series of realignments within the system. In the case of France, for instance, the policy was essentially an inflationary growth strategy, in which the value of the French franc was lowered a few times in an attempt to restore the international competitiveness of French exports. A similar trend was observed for Italy. In a scheme such as EMU—with irrevocably fixed conversion rates among national currencies—such adaptations are no longer feasible. The shift from the EMS to EMU, then, has further sharpened the loss of national monetary sovereignty, implying that macroeconomic shocks can no longer be absorbed by adaptations of the exchange rate. Whereas the EMS had already greatly limited national monetary sovereignty, the shift to EMU has abolished this instrument. The only remaining effective tool for governments to use to steer their economies, apart from indirect influence via the ECB, and possibly the Ecofin Council, is fiscal policy, which is, however, constrained by the collective provisions contained in the SGP.

The function of a currency as an international unit of account, in its nonofficial use, also refers to invoicing practices. For example, at present, the US dollar is very widely used for international trade invoicing. In exchanges with actors in developing countries, generally, either the currency of the industrialized partner country or the US dollar is used. Moreover, the US dollar is widely utilized as a vehicle currency (that is, for the denomination and settlement of trade between countries without involving the United States). Additionally, primary commodities are traditionally invoiced in either dollars or the pound sterling.

Hence, US traders enjoy an advantage by being able to invoice in their domestic currency, which means they automatically forgo exchange-rate risks. Similarly, in the framework of the EMS, an increasing share of intracommunity trade was invoiced in German marks, the share evidently being largest for trade that involved Germany. A country's share of imports invoiced in a foreign country's domestic currency generally exceeds its respective share in exports. This is largely due to the fact that imports contain an automatic hedge against exchange-rate risk because domestic prices of imports are adaptable, but such a hedge does not exist for exports. As a general rule, the more stable a national currency and the lower its inflation rate, the more attractive is its use for international trade invoicing. The ECB's low-inflation priority may therefore strengthen the euro's attractiveness in this regard. Additionally, the larger the total volume of trade invoiced and settled in a specific currency, the lower the effects of single actions on its overall value.

With respect to currency invoicing patterns, earlier developments regarding the German mark may indicate possible future trends for the euro. In the course of the 1980s, little change occurred in German export invoicing with respect to the relative shares of the German mark, the US dollar, the British pound sterling, and other currencies as the denomination of exports (with the exception of a modest increase in the use of the Japanese yen). By comparison, with respect to German imports, the US dollar's share decreased from 32.3 percent in 1980 to 22.0 percent in 1987, whereas the share of the German mark increased from 43.0 to 52.7 percent during the same years, paralleled by a moderate increase in the share of the yen and a decrease in the share of the pound sterling.[4]

In this phase, the German mark was backed by relatively lower inflation rates compared with its EMS partners. Crucial for the German mark's increasing share in currency invoicing was its price stability as compared to other currencies. In order to accept German imports being denominated in German marks, traders needed to trust the currency's stability (as similarly holds with respect to private international investment).

In an international comparison, data before German reunification and the 1992–1993 currency turmoil, during a period of EMS stability, may indicate some further possible effects. In 1988, as compared to 1980, invoicing in German marks remained relatively stable for German exports, with a modest decrease from 82.3 to 81.5 percent of the total. By contrast, the share of German mark invoicing for German imports rose considerably, from 43 percent to 52.6 percent between 1980 and 1988. This phenomenon can also be seen for the French franc (which experienced a moderate decline in its share of exports invoiced in the domestic currency, but a comparatively sharp increase, from 33.1 to 48.9 percent, in the share of its imports). The same trend holds for Italy. By contrast, the share of UK exports invoiced in the pound sterling declined considerably in the course of the 1980s, from 76 percent of its exports in 1980 to 57 percent in 1988. However, the share of imports denominated in the pound sterling remained relatively stable. The United States, during these years, experienced few effects either in terms of exports or imports denominated in US dollars. However, an increasing role in trade invoicing for both exports and imports can be seen for the Japanese yen (mainly reflecting an increasing share of trade invoiced in yen within the Asian region).

Trade invoicing in the framework of the EMS largely rested on the reputation of the domestic currencies, notably in terms of domestic price-level stability. However, the EMS may additionally have contributed to the use of these currencies—for instance, the French franc— by allowing them to borrow credibility from the German Bundesbank and by providing a framework for a relatively high degree of exchange-rate stability (reducing traders' exchange-rate risk). EMU provides this credibility for all Eurosystem states.

The significance of both the US dollar and European currencies in international invoicing practices can also be discerned on the basis of later figures. In 1992, currencies of the 15 EU member states as of 1995 were used in 31 percent of total world trade, compared to 48 percent for the US dollar and 5 percent for the yen.[5] The European Commission has estimated that, for the same year, about 15 percent of total EU exports were invoiced in US dollars. Globally, however, the share of trade denominated in US dollars is high not least because many raw materials, including oil, are denominated in US dollars.[6] Javad Yarjani estimates that by the late 1990s more than 80 percent of all foreign-exchange transactions, and half of all world exports, were denominated in US dollars.[7]

Another factor encouraging the international use of a currency is the relative share of its own domestic region in global trade. For the EU currently, this share is considerable and can be expected to grow in the future. Collignon and Mundschenk (1999: 3) indicate, on the basis of data provided by the Bank for International Settlements (BIS), that the share of EU states in total world exports was 14.7 percent in 1996 (excluding intra-EU trade transactions), compared to 15.2 percent for the United States.

Hence, the size of the "domestic" economy backing the euro is considerable and will grow significantly in the future as an effect of the 2004 EU enlargement. The large share of EU trade in global commerce additionally supports the use of the euro in future trade invoicing. Because the relative shares of trade from most EU neighbors—including the members of the EFTA, remaining non-EU states in Eastern Europe, and states in northern Africa—are highest with the EU, the incentive to use the euro for trade denomination in these regions is further enhanced.

Evidently, non-EMU EU states will be induced, due to their strong trade links with the EU, to denominate an increasing share of their trade in euros (especially since denomination in German marks or, for instance, in French francs is no longer possible). Hence, in regions strongly involved in trade with the EU, the US dollar may partially be replaced by the euro for trade invoicing and payments. Rather unlikely, by contrast, appears to be the use of the euro in either the Asian region—where the yen appears to be increasingly taking on the role of a regional numéraire—or regions geographically close to the United States, including Latin America. Although the EU has strong trade links with the United States—the United States being its largest trade partner—it is less attractive for US traders, due to exchange-rate risks, to denominate exports in euros (whereas an increasing share of invoicing in euros may be expected for US imports, especially exports from EMU member states).

In the framework of the EMS, at least until the 1992–1993 currency turmoil, the Nordic countries, generally, pegged their domestic currencies to the ECU. Switzerland also had de facto pegged its currency to the German mark and now conducts a monetary policy that is still strongly oriented toward the euro. Several of the new EU states have pegged their domestic currencies to the euro. As the ECB emphasizes, this strategy is compatible with the prospect of future EMU membership.[8] Clearly, an orientation of their monetary policies toward the euro is paramount for the ten new EU members as of 2004.

Weaker international currencies generally peg to either a single strong currency or to a basket. In recent decades, there was a trend for several developing countries to shift from pegging to one currency to pegging to a currency basket in order to reduce exchange-rate risk. The attractiveness of pegging to the euro increases with both the countries' relative trade shares with the EU and price stability in the euro area.

States not belonging to EMU, but close to the euro area in geographic terms—either EU or non-EU states—have strong incentives to peg the value of their domestic currencies to the euro. One possible option is to join the exchange-rate arrangement that has succeeded the EMS, the ERM II. The ERM II can be used by new EU states, for example, as preparation for future EMU membership.[9]

Among the countries that have pegged their domestic currency to the euro since 1999 are Cyprus, Denmark, Iceland, but also, for example, Cape Verde. By comparison, Latvia pegged its currency to SDRs (as did, for example, Myanmar, Saudi Arabia, and the United Arab Emirates). Malta has pegged its domestic currency to a currency basket consisting of euros, US dollars, and the pound sterling. In the Slovak Republic and in Slovenia, the euro was used informally as a reference currency. Several African countries, especially those with former ties to France, have now also pegged their domestic currency to the euro.[10]

A second major role for the euro in global monetary affairs is as a means of payment. In this function, it can, for instance, be used to settle international trade debts and to discharge international financial obligations. In terms of its private use, the considerations with respect to the euro as a unit of account are also largely valid regarding its potential ability to meet international financial obligations. In its official use, it can serve as an instrument for balance-of-payment financing and as an intervention device in foreign-exchange markets. The following sections look mainly at developments of European currencies for intervention purposes in foreign-exchange markets.

Whereas the Bretton Woods system was largely dominated by the US dollar as a means of payment, just as the time of the gold standard between approximately 1870 and 1914 was dominated by the pound sterling, the current international monetary system increasingly has the character of a multicurrency system. This trend could already be seen, for example, with respect to interventions in the framework of the EMS and respective activities of the US Federal Reserve in international foreign-exchange markets. Developments regarding the currency distribution used for intervention in the EMS are illustrative of this trend: intervention within the EMS increasingly occurred with EMS currencies (with a gradually increasing share of German mark), at the expense of the US dollar. From 1979 to 1982, the share of US dollars used in EMS interventions was 71.5 percent, but the share declined to 53.7 percent from 1983 through 1985 and to 26.3 percent from 1986 through 1989. By comparison, the share of EMS currencies used for intervention within the EMS was 27.2 percent from 1979 through 1982 (with 23.7 percent for the German mark), 43.5 percent from 1983 through 1985 (39.4 percent for the German mark), and 71.7 percent from 1986 through 1989 (with 59 percent for the German mark).[11]

However, the German mark lost ground compared to the yen in this period as an intervention currency used by the US Federal Reserve and the US Treasury. The German mark's average share in interventions was 89.7 percent from 1979 through 1983 (compared to 10.3 percent for the yen), but it was 67.9 percent from 1983 through 1985 (32.1 percent for the yen), and 57.5 percent from 1986 through 1989 (compared to 42.5 percent for the yen).[12] Whereas the role of the German mark as an official means of payment and intervention currency for the EMS strongly increased over time, the mark was used less by the US Federal Reserve to affect the external value of the dollar. The 1992–1993 currency turmoil in the EMS enhanced the attractiveness of the German mark (and the Dutch guilder), at the expense of other ERM currencies, for intervention purposes in the framework of the EMS.

During the 1970s and the 1980s, intervention was quite frequent in order to stabilize (i.e., either raise or suppress) the foreign-exchange rate of the US dollar. For example, in 1973 and 1974, the Bank of Japan intervened to support the external value of the yen as compared to the US dollar. In 1975 through 1977, however, it acted to stem its appreciation.[13] In both 1977 and 1978, the Bundesbank and the US Federal Reserve undertook extensive intervention in an attempt to support the declining value of the US dollar.[14]

Collignon and Mundschenk (1999: 5) emphasize that the potential use of the euro as an intervention currency is strongly related to its function as a pegging currency: countries having their domestic currency pegged to the euro will by necessity use it extensively for intervention purposes. Countries not using a direct peg to the euro, however, can also employ it as a tool for intervention in an effort to meet more informal exchange-rate objectives.

What other indicators exist regarding the use of currencies as a means of payment? The turnover of currencies on foreign-exchange markets provides an indication of the use of national currencies to settle international financial obligations, as can be seen in the development of the German mark, the French franc, and the British pound sterling in relation to the US dollar during the stable phase of the EMS. Use of the German mark in the composition of currency turnover on the New York foreign-exchange market remained relatively stable, with 31.8 percent in 1980 as compared to 32.9 percent in 1989.[15] By contrast, the respective shares of the French franc and the British pound sterling declined considerably, from 6.9 (franc) and 22.7 percent (pound sterling) in 1980, to 3.2 and 14.6, respectively, in 1989. Turnover increased, however, for the Japanese yen (paralleling the increased use of the yen by the US Treasury to intervene in foreign-exchange markets).[16]

In April 1995, the respective shares of these currencies in global gross foreign-exchange turnover were 18.5 percent (German mark), 4.0 percent (French franc), 5.0 percent (British pound sterling), and 12.0 percent (Japanese yen).[17] In 2002, however, the euro was used in 43 percent of all foreign-exchange transactions.[18] These figures indeed illustrate an increased use over time of European currencies, and later the euro, in global exchange markets.

The international use of a currency is also determined by its function as a store of value. On the one hand, individuals can use a currency for private purposes of borrowing and investment. Official actors, by contrast, hold foreign currencies as reserve assets. In terms of its private use, the ECU has been rather attractive for investors: due to the nature of the ECU as a basket currency, ECU international bonds have constituted a diversified portfolio with automatically reduced exchange-rate risk. This character of the ECU had led to a considerable increase in the issue of international ECU-denominated bonds. Between 1986 and 1991, the increase in total volume was from 6.3 billion US dollars to 32.6 billion. In 1991, in fact, ECU international bond issues were a close second to US dollar issues.[19]

The significance of ECU bonds was strongly affected, however, by the 1992–1993 EMS currency turmoil. As measured in billion ECU, the total of ECU bond issues, which had risen to 27.2 by 1991, subsequently dropped to 19.2 (1992), 6.9 (1993), 5.5 (1994), and 5.6 (1995).[20] As these numbers illustrate, instability within the EMS significantly affected the trust of international investors in the ECU. This sensitivity can be assumed to similarly apply to the role of the euro in international private investment, providing a considerable incentive for the ECB to maintain monetary and price-level stability.

In September 1997, the currencies of the fifteen EU member states were used in the denomination of 41.9 percent of all international bond offerings (compared to 45.1 percent for the US dollar).[21] The share of

European currencies in the denomination of Latin American external debt in 1997 was 12 percent (compared to 67 percent for the US dollar and 11 percent for the Japanese yen). Regarding denomination of Asian external debt in the same year, the share of European currencies was 33 percent, compared to 46 percent for the US dollar and 16 percent for the Japanese yen.[22] Recent data for the Asian region indicate an increasing share of the yen in the denomination of governments' external debt. Similarly, the euro may be used increasingly in the future to denominate developing countries' official debt in regions close to Europe geographically or in areas where ties of trade or foreign aid to EMU states are strong for historical reasons.

The current share of the US dollar in international reserves is rather extensive, although a declining trend can be discerned. For example, the US dollar was used in 80 percent of total identified official reserve holdings in 1968, 85.1 percent in 1975, 60.2 percent in 1989, and 57.3 percent in 1995. Trends for the German mark, by comparison, were the opposite, with a share in total identified official holdings of 1.5 percent in 1968, 6.6 percent in 1975, 19.3 percent in 1989, and 20.1 percent in 1995.[23] Accordingly, at the end of 1995, relative shares in global official foreign-exchange reserves were 56.4 percent for the US dollar and 25.8 percent for the then fifteen EU member states.[24] However, at the end of 1997, the former European domestic currencies accounted for 19.6 percent of official reserves, the US dollar for 57.1 percent, and the yen for 4.9 percent.[25] The establishment of the euro, evidently, abolished holdings by international central banks in national European currencies (with the exception, for example, of the pound sterling and of the Swiss franc). For the EU members participating in EMU, official foreign reserves are now pooled and managed by the ESCB (in accordance with Article 105.2 of the original TEU).

The share of the former European currencies used in the euro area decreased somewhat as a result of technical adjustment linked to the introduction of the euro. One reason for the decrease is that from January 1, 1999, onward reserves in the national banks of Eurosystem states that had previously been denominated in other members' domestic currencies have technically become domestic assets.[26] In 2002, the euro accounted for 13 percent of world currency reserves, compared to 68 percent for the US dollar.[27]

These figures on the composition of official reserves indicate that a global multicurrency system was already in existence toward the end of the twentieth century. The use of currencies as official reserve assets is one indication of a gradual transformation of a hegemonic global economic and monetary structure, although the US dollar is still dominant in global official reserve holdings.

When the yen, based on Japan's new monetary policy oriented toward price stability, gained attractiveness as an international currency, Japan feared an international role for the yen, which implied a partial loss of control over domestic monetary policy. The German Bundesbank, too, has supported an international role of the German mark only with reluctance. However, the international role of both currencies has significantly increased over time. The ECB also emphasizes price stability and does not seem to actively promote the euro's role in the world. The more the euro is used by non-EU countries, however, the larger the privileges for traders based in the euro area.

On the basis of current data, it is difficult to forecast what role the euro might play in international financial and monetary relations in the future. After all, this role will depend on various factors, among them how monetary policy will be conducted in the United States and within the Eurosystem. Political factors, including the stability of the region, will also determine the currency's potential use.

The establishment of EMU on the basis of an institutional setup independent from political pressures, and the likelihood that the significance of the EU may increase in both economic and political terms in the future, suggest the possibility that the euro may indeed become an important player in global monetary relations in the future. Is it going to rival the US dollar? This is a difficult question to answer. International use of one currency may provide significant advantages to domestic users, while another strong international currency, may be much less beneficial for the incumbent monetary actor. However, the political and economic stability of the euro area, which includes both Western and Eastern Europe, will likely provide advantages to non-EU actors, including US businesses and investors.

With the considerable enlargement of the EU in 2004, the economic and demographic area of the EU has expanded significantly.[28] Many of the new EU states are on the road to economic prosperity, although they still lag behind the GDP rates of their western counterparts. The gap is, however, less considerable when relative wealth is measured in terms of Purchasing Power Parities (PPP) rather than GDP per capita. Respective figures are given in Table 6.3.

Among the EU-25, variation regarding GDP per capita rates (i.e., the dispersion of these rates around their average value), with a standard deviation of euro 12.300 compared to the average for the EU-25 of euro 19.400, is relatively pronounced. Variation expressed in terms of PPPs is

Table 6.3 GDP per Capita of the EU Member States, 2003

	GDP per capita (euro thousands)	GDP per capita (PPP[a] thousands)
Austria	27.9	26.4
Belgium	26.0	25.8
Cyprus	*15.9*	*18.4*
Czech Republic	*7.9*	*16.0*
Denmark	34.9	27.1
Estonia	*5.9*	*10.7*
Finland	27.3	24.2
France	25.3	25.0
Germany	25.8	23.8
Greece	13.9	17.5
Hungary	*7.2*	*13.4*
Ireland	33.8	29.3
Italy	22.4	23.5
Latvia	*4.2*	*10.0*
Lithuania	*4.7*	*10.2*
Luxembourg	53.3	46.9
Malta	*10.9*	*16.4*
Netherlands	28.0	26.4
Poland	*4.8*	*10.2*
Portugal	12.4	16.4
Slovak Republic	*5.4*	*11.3*
Slovenia	*12.3*	*17.0*
Spain	18.2	21.0
Sweden	29.8	25.4
UK	26.6	26.1
Average	19.4	20.7
Standard deviation	12.3	8.3

Source: Data from European Central Bank (2005: 38); own calculations.
Notes: New EU states as of 2004 presented in italics.
[a]PPP is a measure used to eliminate effects of price-level differences between countries. It reflects differences in purchasing power, for example, of households. The measure is obtained by a comparison of domestic price levels for a basket of comparable goods and services that are representative of domestic consumption patterns.

indeed lower (with a standard deviation of 8.300 PPPs compared to an average for the EU-25 of 20.700). Hence, purchasing power in several of the new EU states is still below the relative wealth of other EU states, but the gap is not as considerable when measured in purchasing power as it is in terms of GDP per capita. In view of rapid economic growth, significant restructuring, and modernization of their domestic economies, there is little doubt that several of the current Central and Eastern European EU states will soon grow into wealthier states based on modern technologies and infrastructure. Whereas it is probable that EU enlargement and the increase in the geographic size of the euro area may lead to some initial management challenges—not least regarding institutional effectiveness and the ECB's adherence to its overall mandate—there is little doubt that future prosperity in an enlarged EU area may further strengthen the potential of the euro. The difficulties regarding nonharmonized business cycles in the euro area remain, as does the lack of authority of the EU in issues regarding taxation and fiscal policy. But considering the potential for economic growth, shares in global trade, demographic figures, and a high degree of political stability, prospects for an extended euro area are certainly considerable.

In view of the growth of economic power in Asia, notably China's demographic and economic potential, a novel, possibly tripolar monetary and economic global structure cannot be ruled out for the not too distant future. It might then revolve around the poles of the United States, Asia (notably Japan and China), and the EU, possibly paralleling a multipower structure in global politics.

Europe's 1992 internal market program has forced European economies to restructure and abandon remaining economic barriers to trade. While in the short term this caused economic hardship, including high unemployment rates (see Tables 5.1 and 5.2), integration and market liberalization may be expected to create economic gains in the medium- and long-term future. It will certainly not be easy for states in Central and Eastern Europe to adapt to the regulations and provisions of the EU's common market, and even less to the ones of EMU. But the path of economic development of some new EU states, including the Baltic states, Poland, Hungary, and the Czech Republic, is impressive. Maintaining this dynamic, and eventually joining EMU, can only reinforce the weight of the EU economy and, due to the size and potential of this market, strengthen the leverage of EMU in global markets.

Sovereign states often have difficulty accepting a loss of autonomy as an inevitable result of exchange-rate coordination.[29] Fundamental to this is the trade-off described earlier by Mundell (1960) between policy autonomy and exchange-rate stability existing for all but one state, the state holding the numéraire currency, within an international monetary system. In the Bretton Woods system, this currency was the US dollar. In the Snake and the EMS, it was the German mark.[30] How will the creation of the common currency influence international monetary relations?

The provisions of EMU suggest that the predominant goal of the ECB is to maintain price stability—with some factors rendering this task difficult in practice—but possibly at the expense of some global exchange-rate stability.

The concern that the euro might rival the US dollar[31] is reflected in the past policies of US administrations toward European integration more generally, despite a usually supportive rhetoric.[32] On the one hand, an integrated Europe appeared to be attractive especially for the stability it could generate in the region, in both political and economic terms. In economic terms, however, these benefits would be greatest if the area was open for international business interests, not a "Fortress Europe" but an open internal market, based on free trade and liberal patterns of exchange. The same reasoning is likely to apply to monetary integration. If the merging of EMU currencies leads to the elimination of transaction costs for traders and investors both within the EU and outside it, the creation of the euro and EMU appear to be beneficial. If monetary policy were to be dominated by political interests, however, and political rationales were to determine the external value of the euro, for example, European monetary integration would constitute a threat to outsiders. The European experience, as Barry Eichengreen contends, supports those suggesting that stable and extensive trade relations are an important prerequisite for a smooth functioning of the international monetary system.[33] Historically, attempts to stabilize international monetary relations abound. When they were successful, they usually contributed to economic prosperity and expansion for the participating states. The euro, if these circumstances prevail, may indeed be seen as a stabilizing factor in global monetary and financial affairs.

Current developments appear to indicate that, indeed, the model of the German mark and of the Bundesbank have influenced the character of the euro and the ECB: these institutions were largely built on the example of the rather successful experience of German monetary policy during the last decades of the twentieth century. As far as the signs appear to point now, the euro, although largely shaped on the basis of political agreement, may actually be steered not by those political interests but by an independently operating ECB.

Market pressures and the conduct of domestic monetary policies, in the end, determine both the level and significance of a currency. Hence, the future role of the euro will, to a large extent, be determined by the character of monetary policies conducted, notably in the United States and in the EU. Cooperation between two or more international currencies is certainly conceivable, and there may not be a need for a truly hierarchical structure in which one international currency is at the top of a respective global pyramid.[34] Political stability, in addition to prudent monetary policies, will provide the basis for the international significance of these currencies. By comparison to the US Federal Reserve and to the ECB, however, the Japanese central bank has shown reluctance to let the yen assume a more important role as an international currency. The main two actors regarding global monetary affairs, in the medium-term future, therefore appear to be the US Federal Reserve and the ECB.

Regarding prospects for international currency stability, however, it might well be that there is a certain trade-off between intrabloc stabilization and interbloc volatility.[35] This implies that Europe's increasing emphasis on a monetary policy beneficial to the euro area might, in combination with the growth of the EU market, lead to a growing trend in European policy of benign neglect. In this sense, the creation of EMU might stabilize monetary policies in Europe but not necessarily add to prospects for global currency stabilization.

Notes

1. Information provided in this chapter is partially based on Hosli (1998).
2. Trade diversion is measured as the shift from a low-cost external source to a higher-cost partner source due to the creation of the customs union, i.e., the abolishment of tariffs on intracommunity trade and the creation of a common external tariff. For early analyses of this topic, see Viner (1950) and Balassa (1961).
3. See Hosli (1998: 179).
4. See Tavlas (1993), Hosli (1998).
5. Flowers and Lees (2002: 128).
6. See Weinrichter (2000: 31).
7. Yarjani (2002: 1).
8. European Central Bank (2004).
9. Ibid.
10. For a respective overview of exchange rate regimes involving the euro, see Collignon and Mundschenk (1999: 6).
11. Tavlas (1993: 573).
12. Ibid., based on data from the Federal Reserve Bank of New York and the Deutsche Bundesbank.
13. Eichengreen (1996: 143).
14. Ibid.
15. Tavlas (1993: 575).
16. Ibid.
17. Flowers and Lees (2002: 133).
18. Beber (2003: 76).

19. Hosli (1998: 185).

20. Ibid.

21. Flowers and Lees (2002: 133).

22. Figures for Latin American and Asian external debt are from Flowers and Lees (2002), pp. 140 and 142, based on data provided by the Union Bank of Switzerland.

23. Peters (1996: 513).

24. Flowers and Lees (2002: 128).

25. Collignon and Mundschenk (1999: 4).

26. Ibid.

27. Beber (2003: 76).

28. Enlargement by ten new EU states in May 2004 has added 74.7 million people to the 381.7 million of the formerly 15 EU states. This amounts to an increase by about 20 percent. By comparison, the 2004 enlargement added a GDP of 436 billion to the existing one (15 member states) of 9.296 billion euros. This is an increase of about 5 percent. See *ECB Monthly Bulletin,* February 2004.

29. Heisenberg (1999: 4).

30. Ibid. (17–18).

31. See Cohen (1998).

32. See Henning and Padoan (2000).

33. Eichengreen (1996: 153).

34. For a description of possible hierarchies of currencies, see Cohen (1998).

35. Collignon and Mundschenk (1999: 10).

7

Conclusions

The creation of the euro, largely on the basis of political momentum, may indeed turn out to be one of the most significant developments in the recent history of international monetary relations. Without doubt, EMU is now an essential actor in the international political economy, not least due to the EU's weight in global trade relations and forthcoming EMU enlargement. This book contends that the euro may indeed be a fairly stable and, therefore major, world currency in the future of global financial and monetary affairs.

Since the creation of the euro, the new European currency has experienced some ups and downs, mainly regarding the level of its exchange rate. The external value of the euro was disappointing to many shortly after EMU was introduced: from an initial exchange rate with the US dollar of 1 euro to 1.17 dollars, the value of the euro subsequently experienced a slow but steady decrease. Between January 1, 1999, and early 2002, it depreciated against the US dollar by about 25 percent.[1] This decrease led many observers to doubt whether the currency was stable and whether international actors could trust its potential. In the more recent past, the external value of the euro has risen quite significantly, however, reaching an exchange rate with the US dollar of about 1 euro to 1.2 dollars in the winter of 2004 and exceeding 1 euro to 1.3 dollars in the beginning of 2005.

Although empirical evidence from the recent past illustrates that the euro may indeed be on a fairly sound basis, it is facing challenges. EMU is criticized because it does not yet constitute an OCA and because it is based on undemocratic foundations. Considerable challenges are linked to EU—and hence EMU—enlargement and the temptation of political actors to press for an active exchange-rate and growth policy.

The ECB is hardly influenced by political pressures. This orientation is firmly anchored in its statutes. However, both the EU and EMU are entities in flux, not least due to significant EU enlargement. While governments and special interest groups appear to have few means to influence the monetary policies of Europe's new central bank, the ECB has been criticized extensively by such groups, especially when the euro performed weakly on global exchange markets. In some sense, however, this criticism might be a healthy sign regarding its independence from politics.

What are the origins of the euro? Why was EMU created? What are the prospects for the euro in the future? An overview of the history of regional monetary cooperation in Europe, as outlined in the beginning of this book, reveals that regional monetary integration, especially among the highly trade-dependent and open economies of EC member states, was largely necessitated by the provisions of the CAP and plans to create a common market in the EC. Economic integration and economic interdependence rendered exchange-rate volatility among EC states costly and undesirable.

The breakdown of the Bretton Woods regime in the early 1970s sparked a series of efforts to establish a monetary union among EC states or at least to create schemes that would allow for exchange-rate stability in the region. Following the currency Snake, regional exchange-rate cooperation resulted in the creation of the EMS in 1979. Although based on pressures stemming from global markets, incentives leading to the establishment of these regional monetary arrangements seemed to be mostly of a political nature.

It is difficult to establish with certainly what the effects of the EMS have been on convergence in monetary, and macroeconomic, policy behavior of EC states. Convergence of ideas regarding effective monetary policies may have been as important as the institutional structure of the EMS, which explicitly encouraged such convergence. Clearly, the Bundesbank played a central role within the EMS[2]—in some ways comparable to the role of the US Federal Reserve within the Bretton Woods regime—on the basis of its well-respected anti-inflation policy. Its own adherence to strict interpretations of the primacy of price stability is largely to be understood on the basis of undesired effects and bad recollections of high inflation experienced during the times of the Weimar Republic in particular.

Within the EMS, credibility was largely borrowed from the Bundesbank by other, partially less politically independent, central banks. Like the Bretton Woods system, the EMS was a system of fixed but adjustable exchange rates. Political agreement was needed for modifications of bilateral exchange rates, but revaluations or devaluations of domestic currencies were largely induced by market pressures.

The EMS clearly was essential to the prospect of establishing EMU, not least because monetary convergence experienced during the existence of the EMS made the prospect of monetary union in Europe more realistic. The convergence of monetary, and partially fiscal, indicators, together with the perception of the EMS as a mechanism strengthening exchange-rate stability in Europe, made EMU seem both desirable and feasible. In addition, the goal of finalizing the EU's internal market by 1992 created pressures to abolish remaining transaction costs in trade among EU states. Currency volatility was potentially disruptive economically for the trade-dependent EU members.

Although economic recession hit in the early 1990s, the effects of adverse economic conditions were not as disturbing as those witnessed in the 1970s following the two major oil price shocks. Plans for monetary union, this time, were not abandoned.

Macroeconomic and monetary convergence occurred within the EMS, especially regarding inflation rates and long-term interest rates. However, different schools of thought attribute relatively more importance to selected factors that may have contributed to this development and to respective preparations for EMU. Some argue that this convergence was largely due to the role of new ideas and the actual emergence of a neoliberal policy consensus.[3] Others posit, that, for the most part, these results reflected the preferences and bargaining strengths of different parties involved in the respective IGCs.[4] Several authors agree that Germany was highly influential in the intergovernmental negotiations on the provisions for EMU and that the preferences of the German negotiators are, to a great extent, reflected in the final provisions on monetary union.[5] The road to the creation of EMU was, however, marked by significant hurdles. In 1992 and 1993, Western European financial markets were shaken by a series of currency crises. The EMS exchange-rate mechanism, operating with narrow fluctuation margins in order to contain currency volatility among EC states, appeared to be untenable and, finally, bilateral fluctuation margins among most EMS currencies were widened significantly (from 2.25 percent to 15 percent). At this point, the currencies were almost floating. In fact, one of the major reasons for the currency crises may have been the abolishment of remaining capital controls, as contained in the first stage of EMU institutionalization.[6] High volumes of international capital transactions and rapid market reactions put relatively weak currencies under heavy speculative pressure. In addition, many European states faced economic downturn in the beginning of the 1990s. These factors contributed to making EMU appear, in the mid-1990s, to be a rather difficult endeavor.

Several EU member states participated in what seemed to be a race to be in the first group of EMU members. This competition was made more difficult by prevailing adverse economic circumstances. Some of the short-term economic difficulties may in fact have been created by the very restructuring of national economies in the framework of the 1992 program (the internal market program): Allowing for increased economic efficiency within the common market required the abolishment of several existing tools to protect national economies. Remaining nontariff barriers to trade, including discriminatory product regulations and practices to protect domestic producers, had to be gradually removed. It is not surprising that this would cause economic hardship in the short term, despite expected gains for the future. Increasing unemployment rates were part of this development.[7]

The TEU, or Maastricht Treaty,[8] defined five convergence criteria EU member states would need to meet in order to qualify for EMU membership. The decision on who would be able to join was to be made by political bodies of the EU during the course of 1997.[9] The convergence criteria stipulated that member states should have budget deficits no higher than 3 percent of their GDP. This goal appeared to be relatively easily attainable during the economically prosperous and booming years of the late 1980s, but not during the economic downturn in the early 1990s. Recession leads to lower government earnings due to decreased tax receipts, and more public funds need to be spent providing for unemployment and social benefits. This is especially true in the context of the relatively elaborate social welfare systems characterizing many Western European states, notably those located in northern Europe.

Somewhat unexpected were Germany's difficulties in meeting these fiscal targets. Whereas West Germany had been a model for others regarding the soundness of its economic and monetary policies for decades after World War II and had played a central role within the EMS, German unification in the early 1990s induced heavy pressures on German public finances.[10] Similarly, pressures were considerable for France to maintain a relatively modest budget deficit. Later aggravation of these problems led to what amounted to a small political crisis within the EU in the fall of 2003 and a considerable easing of the rules of the SGP.

After the provisions for EMU had been anchored in the TEU, several EU states faced difficulties not only with budget deficits but also regarding debt ratios. A second convergence criterion stipulated that general government debt should not exceed 60 percent of GDP or that, at least, a considerable decrease in the ratio of debt to GDP would need to be achieved to allow for euro area membership. Among the EMS countries with extensive government debts were Belgium and Italy.

As they prepared for EMU membership, some governments clearly used the "outside pressures" to introduce policy reforms they long intended to undertake but could not afford to do politically. In a sense, the provisions of the TEU and the pressure in public opinion to be in the first group of EMU countries and not be left out, made the EMU plan serve as a useful scapegoat to allow for unpopular, but much needed, domestic policy reforms. This scapegoat, however, was not always sufficient to allow for implementation of the necessary fiscal and monetary provisions. Complying with the given convergence criteria turned out to be very difficult in practice for several EC states. To meet the criteria, some states used rather creative accounting mechanisms, measures that were strongly criticized in turn.[11]

After considerable doubts about whether EMU would start on time and whether the convergence criteria would be interpreted in a strict way, EMU began on January 1, 1999. In fact, considering the sheer magnitude of this enterprise, the initiation of EMU was impressively smooth. The replacement of national currencies by the euro during the course of the year 2002 had been well prepared and was skillfully orchestrated. Despite a clear reluctance to abandon national currencies in large segments of the populations of several EU states, the introduction of the euro, in technical terms, went very smoothly. The supply of the new currency worked well, and money and vending machines, generally, made the switch to the new currency in time. Double listing of amounts in both euros and domestic currencies in stores and banks and on salary slips for months, for example, had prepared European citizens for the big step of the changeover to EMU.

Despite the elegant beginning in technical terms and the resulting smooth operative transition to EMU, the euro appeared not to be doing well on international markets after its introduction. It gradually lost value compared to major international currencies, notably the US dollar. Similarly, it weakened compared to, for example, the British pound sterling and the Swiss franc. Was this a sign that the ECB did not operate well? Was the EU, after all, not ready for EMU? Did the ECB make significant policy mistakes?

After what appeared to be a rather slow start, reflected in the euro's depressed value in international currency markets, its position in international monetary relations started to improve. In fact, the euro gained strength considerably, clearly surpassing parity with the US dollar in 2003. While this certainly was an unfavorable development for European export interests—but much better news for US exporters operating on European markets, for example—attitudes towards the ECB and its management appeared to change. The perception of a strong euro, as adverse as its effects may have been for European exporters, appeared to lend credibility to the ECB's policies.

How do the ECB and the ESCB work in practice? How are these institutions organized, and who is represented in them? It is important to know how these institutions are structured in order to understand the ways in which monetary policy is conducted for the euro area. The ECB was headed by Willem Duisenberg, a former president of the Dutch central bank, until November 2003. Since then, it has been chaired by Jean-Claude Trichet, a former president of the central bank of France. Two institutions are central to the ECB's operation: the executive board, consisting of the ECB's president and vice-president and four additional monetary policy experts, and the governing council, consisting of the ECB executive board members and of the governors of euro-area central banks. In order to deal with macroeconomic and monetary policy challenges within the EU, a general council includes central bank governors of EU states that are not yet in the Eurosystem. For example, the new EU states as of May 2004 have obtained seats in the ECB general council, but not yet in the governing council.

As plans for EMU were being finalized, it was clear that some EU states (notably the United Kingdom, Denmark, and Sweden) wished not to join the first group of countries starting out with EMU. These EU states, partially due to intensive domestic political debates, stay out of the EMU construct. A new version of the earlier ERM, the ERM II, was set up in order to keep the currencies of EMU outsiders within predefined fluctuation bands with the euro. Again, membership in the ERM II reflects a deliberate strategy to control exchange-rate volatility in Europe and is now also used as an intermediate step for new EU states before entering EMU.

What are the prospects for the euro in the future? Will the new currency eventually "rival" the US dollar? Or is it doomed to "fail" on global currency markets? To what extent is the euro likely to be used in international monetary relations as a unit of account, a means of payment, or a store of value?

Critics, mainly from an economic perspective, point to the fact that the EU is not (yet) an OCA. This implies that labor mobility within the EU is still rather low, as is wage flexibility. According to such critics, major economic shocks to the system might put serious strains on EMU and possibly either force the new monetary union to collapse or, even more dramatically, initiate political conflict within the EU. More optimistic forecasts, however, point to the potentially beneficial effects of the euro's establishment. For example, EMU may help stabilize European economies, both in Western and Eastern Europe. The ECB's primacy of price stability, allowing for low inflation in the medium and long term for Europe's economies, may prove to be a considerable asset for global traders and investors. EMU strengthens the EU's internal market by further eliminating transaction costs (mainly those linked to costs of exchanging currencies and of the lack of transparency when prices are denoted in different currencies). The introduction of the euro, therefore, facilitates trade and increases information for consumers, irrespective of their geographical origin. In this sense, supporters of the euro view the introduction of Europe's new currency as a beneficial development.

Were the critical voices in the times of a low euro exchange rate justified? Does a low exchange rate imply that a currency is weak? There is a vast (economic) literature about exchange rates and the advantages and disadvantages of relative exchange-rate strength or weakness. From a political-economy perspective, it is clear that a depreciated value of a currency benefits some actors while it is a disadvantage for others. Accordingly, different domestic actors have different preferences regarding the level (and stability) of exchange rates.[12] Expressed in simple terms, a depreciated value of the euro is certainly beneficial for European exporters, since their products are then competitive compared to those of other world economic actors, including US producers. By contrast, a depreciated external value of the euro is not desirable for actors holding assets in euros. Whereas it is pleasant for US or Japanese tourists, for example, to travel in Europe when the external value of the euro is low, European tourists in the United States are less excited. Clearly, there are always winners and losers with specific levels of an exchange rate.[13]

During the times of a depressed euro, there was criticism of the first ECB president, Willem Duisenberg, and his team. Some of this criticism may have been justified, but it has to be stressed that the objective of the ECB is not to maintain a stable exchange rate but to maintain price stability in the euro area.[14] Empirical evidence suggests that this overall goal of the ECB has largely been fulfilled in practice. To some extent, criticism of the depreciated value of the euro was undeserved. After all, phases of depreciation of the US dollar, for example,[15] have not necessarily been interpreted as a policy failure on the part of the US Federal Reserve.

Whether a currency will eventually enhance stability in the global monetary order and whether it will play a significant role in international financial affairs depends on several factors. This book contends that the euro may well be both a stable factor in global financial relations and a significant international currency in the future. It would only be a true rival of the US dollar in a negative sense, however, if it were to be used as a political means to achieve economic ends (for example, if the external value of the euro would be determined by political forces and used as a tool to boost EU exports). But a currency's credibility can only be established globally if its value is determined by market forces, if it is steered by an independent central bank, and if the economic weight of the region it represents is large enough to make it a significant actor in world trade. A precondition for a positive, stabilizing role for the euro in global financial and commercial affairs is that traders and investors judge the policies of the ECB to be credible. If the ECB's policies appear to be determined by the interests of day-to-day political pressures, possibly as voiced by governmental institutions, the euro is unlikely to establish a long-term reputation of reliability and stability.

An optimistic approach to future monetary relations assumes that cooperation among the major world monetary actors—notably the US Federal Reserve, the central bank of Japan, and the ECB—will be feasible and realistic. This may only hold if relations are not distorted by major international crises of an economic or political nature, however. In addition, it may well be that the creation of the euro will lead to more volatility in currency relations between Europe and the United States, for example.

It is clear that the euro has made its debut into international monetary affairs. Its future cannot be predicted with certainty, not least due to recent challenges to the new currency, including significant widening of EU—and future EMU—membership. But it is clear, as this book demonstrates, that the euro, although partially a political construct, is a fairly stable currency, based on a large demographic and economic basis and characterized by political stability and prosperity. In this sense, the euro has the potential to be a significant world currency, most likely as one major player in today's multipolar global economic and financial system.

Notes

1. Babarinde (2003: 304).
2. See Kennedy (1991), Loedel (1999), Heisenberg (1999).

3. McNamara (1998, 1999), Heisenberg (1999).

4. See Moravcsik (1998); Walsh (2000).

5. See Moravcsik (1998); Walsh (2000).

6. Step I of EMU was completed in the summer of 1990.

7. Another possible reason for high unemployment across Europe and difficulties of EMU is the lack of flexibility of labor markets. This argument is prominent in the literature on OCAs and EMU, with some authors doubting that European economies were really ready for monetary union.

8. The final negotiations on this treaty took place in December 1991 in the city of Maastricht, in the south of the Netherlands, under the Dutch presidency.

9. The decision was to be made by the European Council (which comprises the heads of state or government of the EU) on the basis of a recommendation of the EMI (the precursor of the ECB) and the European Commission.

10. Combined with economic downturn, it became clear that the budget deficit could not be kept under 3 percent. This was true even after the creation of EMU, despite respective arrangements made—notably the SGP—to let EMU members stay under the 3 percent of GDP ceiling for government deficits.

11. See Leblond (2003).

12. This issue is discussed succinctly by Frieden (1991).

13. See Frieden (2002) for an analysis of sectoral interests within EMU concerning the level of the euro exchange rate.

14. The ECB's policy orientation is clearly defended along these lines by Issing (1999).

15. On this, see Spero and Hart (2003).

Acronyms

BEPG	Broad Economic Policy Guidelines
BIS	Bank for International Settlements
CAP	Common Agricultural Policy
CCBG	Committee of Central Bank Governors
CFSP	Common Foreign and Security Policy
CPI	Consumer Price Index
CU	Customs Union
EC	European Community
ECB	European Central Bank
ECJ	European Court of Justice
Ecofin	Council of Ministers of Economics and Finance
ECU	European Currency Unit
EEC	European Economic Community
EFC	Economic and Financial Committee
EFTA	European Free Trade Association
EMA	European Monetary Agreement
EMCF	European Monetary Compensation Fund
EMI	European Monetary Institute
EMS	European Monetary System
EMU	Economic and Monetary Union
EP	European Parliament
EPU	European Political Union
ERM	Exchange Rate Mechanism
ESCB	European System of Central Banks
EU	European Union
EUA	European Unit of Account
EUP	European Payments Union

FTA	Free Trade Agreement
GATT	General Agreement on Tariffs and Trade
GDP	Gross Domestic Product
G-5	Group of Five
G-7	Group of Seven
HICP	Harmonized Index of Consumer Prices
IBRD	International Bank for Reconstruction and Development (World Bank)
IGC	Intergovernmental Conference
IMF	International Monetary Fund
IPE	International Political Economy
ITO	International Trade Organization
OCA	Optimum Currency Area
OECD	Organization for Economic Cooperation and Development
OEEC	Organization for European Economic Cooperation (later OECD)
OMC	Open Method of Coordination
OPEC	Organization of Petroleum Exporting Countries
PPP	Purchasing Power Parities
SDR	Special Drawing Rights
SEA	Single European Act
SGP	Stability and Growth Pact
TEC	Consolidated Treaty of the European Community
TEU	Treaty on European Union ("Maastricht Treaty")

Bibliography

Alesina, Alberto, O. Blanchard, J. Gali, Franesco Giavazzi, and H. Uhlig (2001): Defining a Macroeconomic Framework for the Euro Area. Center for Economic Policy Research (CEPR), London.

Andrews, David M., and Thomas D. Willett (1997): "Financial Interdependence and the State: International Monetary Relations at Century's End." *International Organization* 51, no. 2: 479–511.

Arnold, Christine, Madeleine O. Hosli, and Paul Pennings (2004): Social Policy-Making in the European Union: A New Mode of Governance? Paper presented at the 2004 Conference of Europeanists, March 11–13, Chicago.

Aziz, Nazli (2004): Delegation and the European Central Bank's Democratic Deficit: It Takes Two to Tango. MA Thesis, June, Leiden University.

Babarinde, Olufemi A. (2003): "The Euro Debuts: European Money, Global Money, or Both?" In *International Political Economy: State-Market Relations in the Changing Global Order,* ed. C. Roe Goddard, Patrick Cronin, and Kishore C. Dash, 291–314. Basingstoke, Hampshire: Palgrave Macmillan.

Balassa, Bela (1961): *The Theory of Economic Integration.* Homewood, IL: Irwin.

Baldwin, Richard, E. Berglof, Francesco Giavazzi, and Mika Widgrén (2001a): *Nice Try: Should the Treaty of Nice Be Ratified?* Washington, DC: The Brookings Institution.

Baldwin, Richard, Erik Berglof, Francesco Giavazzi, and Mika Widgrén (2001b): Preparing the ECB for Enlargement. CEPR discussion paper, 6.

Banducci, Susan A., Jeffrey A. Karp, and Peter H. Loedel (2003): "The Euro, Economic Interests and Multi-Level Governance: Examining Support for the Common Currency." *European Journal of Political Research* 42, no. 5: 685–703.

Beber, Massimo (2003), "The European Central Bank in 2002: Waiting for Recovery." *Journal of Common Market Studies* 41: 75–78.

Begg, Iain, ed. (2002): *Europe, Government and Money—Running EMU: The Challenges of Policy Coordination.* London: Federal Trust.

——— (2003): Hard and Soft Economic Policy Coordination under EMU: Problems, Paradoxes and Prospects. Working paper 103, European Institute, London School of Economics and Political Science.

Berman, Sheri, and Kathleen R. McNamara (1999): "Bank on Democracy: Why Central Banks Need Public Oversight." *Foreign Affairs* 78, no. 2: 2–8.

Bernhard, William, and David Leblang (2002): "Political Parties and Monetary Commitments." *International Organization* 56, no. 4: 803–830.

Bernhard, William, J. Lawrence Broz, and William Roberts Clark (2002): "The Political Economy of Monetary Institutions." *International Organization* 56, no. 4: 693–723.

Black, Stanley W. (1993): "The International Use of Currencies." In *International Finance: Contemporary Issues,* ed. Dilip K. Das, 553–565. London: Routledge.

Börzel, Tanja, and Madeleine O. Hosli (2003): "Brussels Between Bern and Berlin: Comparative Federalism Meets the European Union." *Governance* 16, no. 2: 179–202.

Bordo, M., and Barry Eichengreen (1993): *A Retrospective on the Bretton Woods System.* Chicago: University of Chicago Press.

Buiter, Willem H. (1999): "Alice in Euroland." *Journal of Common Market Studies* 37, no. 2: 181–209.

Buiter, Willem H., Giancarlo Corsetti, and Nouriel Roubini (1993): "Excessive Deficits: Sense and Nonsense in the Treaty of Maastricht." *Economic Policy* 16: 57–100.

Cameron, David R. (1992): "The 1992 Initiative: Causes and Consequences." In *Euro-Politics: Institutions and Policymaking in the 'New' European Community,* ed. Alberta Sbragia, 23–74. Washington: Brookings Institution.

——— (1995) "Transnational Relations and the Development of European Economic and Monetary Union." In *Bringing Transnational Relations Back In: Non-State Actors, Domestic Structures and International Institutions,* ed. Thomas Risse-Kappen, 37–78. New York: Cambridge University Press.

Cohen, Benjamin (1977): *Organizing the World's Money.* New York: Basic Books.

——— (1993): "The Triad and the Unholy Trinity: Lessons for the Pacific Rim." In *Pacific Economic Relations in the 1990s,* ed. R. Higgott, R. Leaver, and J. Ravenhill. Boulder, CO: Lynne Rienner.

——— (1998): *The Geography of Money.* Ithaca: Cornell University Press.

——— (2003): "Monetary Governance in a Globalized World." In *International Political Economy: State-Market Relations in the Changing Global Order,* ed. C. Roe Goddard, Patrick Cronin, and Kishore C. Dash, 215–239. Basingstoke, Hampshire: Palgrave Macmillan.

Collignon, Stefan, and Susanne Mundschenk (1999): The Euro as an International Currency (mimeo).

Committee for the Study of Economic and Monetary Union (1989): *Report on Economic and Monetary Union in the European Community.* Brussels: Committee for the Study of EMU, April 12.

Cooper, Scott (1997): Governments Against Independent Central Banks: Explaining German Acceptance of EMU. Paper presented at the annual meeting of the American Political Science Association (APSA), Washington, DC, August 28–31.

Crombez, Christophe (2003): "The Democratic Deficit in the European Union." *European Union Politics* 4, no. 1: 101–120.

Crowley, Patrick M. (2002): "The Institutional Implications of EMU." *Journal of Common Market Studies* 39, no. 3: 385–404.

Das, Dilip K., ed. (1993): *International Finance: Contemporary Issues.* London: Routledge.

De Grauwe, Paul (1989): *International Money: Post-War Trends and Theories.* Oxford: Clarendon Press.

——— (1993): "The Political Economy of Monetary Integration in Europe." *The World Economy* 16, no. 6: 653–661.

——— (2000): "Monetary Policies in the Presence of Asymmetries." *Journal of Common Market Studies* 38, no. 4: 593–612.

——— (2002): "Challenges for Monetary Policy in Euroland." *Journal of Common Market Studies* 40: no. 4, 693–718.

——— (2003): Towards an Intelligent Stability and Growth Pact (mimeo).

Dinan, Desmond (1999): *Ever Closer Union? An Introduction to the European Community,* 2nd ed. Boulder, CO: Lynne Rienner.

——— ed. (2000): *Encyclopedia of the European Union.* Boulder, CO: Lynne Rienner.

Dornbusch, Rudiger (1996): "Euro Fantasies." *Foreign Affairs* 75 (September/October): 110–125.

——— (2000): "Making EMU a Success." *International Affairs* 76, no. 1: 89–110.

Dornbusch, Rudiger, Carlo A. Favero, and Francesco Giavazzi (1998): "The Immediate Challenges for the European Central Bank." In *EMU: Prospects and Challenges for the Euro,* ed. David Begg et al., 15–64. Oxford: Blackwell.

Dyson, Kenneth (1994): *Elusive Union: The Process of Economic and Monetary Union in Europe.* London: Longman.

——— ed. (2002): *European States and the Euro: Europeanization, Variation, and Convergence.* Oxford: Oxford University Press.

Dyson, Kenneth, and Kevin Featherstone (1996): France, EMU and Construction Européenne: Enpowering the Executive, Transforming the State. Paper presented at the Conference "L'Européanisation des Politiques Publiques" (The Europeanization of Public Policies), Paris, June 20–21.

Dyson, Kenneth, and Kevin Featherstone (1999): *The Road to Maastricht: Negotiating Economic and Monetary Union.* Oxford: Oxford University Press.

Dyson, Kenneth, Kevin Featherstone, and George Michalopoulos (1995): "Strapped to the Mast: EC Central Bankers Between Global Financial Markets and Regional Integration." *Journal of European Public Policy* 2, no. 3: 465–487.

Eichengreen, Barry (1987): Hegemonic Stability Theories of the International Monetary System, Working paper no. 2193, Cambridge, MA: National Bureau of Economic Research.

——— (1996): *Globalizing Capital: A History of the International Monetary System.* Princeton: Princeton University Press.

Eichengreen, Barry, and Jeffry Frieden, ed. (1994): *The Political Economy of European Monetary Unification.* Boulder, CO: Westview Press.

Eichengreen, Barry, and Jeffry Frieden (1994): "The Political Economy of European Monetary Unification: An Analytical Introduction." In *The Political*

Economy of European Monetary Unification, ed. Barry Eichengreen and Jeffry Frieden, 1–23. Boulder, CO: Westview Press.

Eichengreen, Barry and Charles Wyplosz (1993): "The Unstable EMS." *Brookings Papers on Economic Activity* 1: 51–143

Elgie, Robert (2002): "Democratic Accountability and Central Bank Independence: Historical and Contemporary, National and European Perspectives." *West European Politics* 21, no. 3: 53–65.

Enderlein, Henrik (2003): Adjusting to EMU: The Impact of Monetary Union on Domestic Fiscal and Wage-Setting Institutions. Paper presented at the 8th International Conference of the European Union Studies Association (EUSA), Nashville, Tennessee, March 27–29.

European Central Bank (2004): Frequently Asked Questions: EU Enlargement and Economic and Monetary Union (EMU). Available at http://www.ecb.int/enlargement/enl_faq_en.htm.

European Central Bank (2005): *Statistics Pocket Book* (January).

European Commission (1990): "One Market, One Money." *European Economy* 44 (October).

European Monetary Institute (1996). *Progress Toward Convergence 1996,* November.

European Parliament (1998): The International Role of the Euro. Available at http://www.europarl.eu.int/workingpapers/econ/101/chap1_en.htm.

Feldstein, Martin (1997a): "The Political Economy of the European Economic and Monetary Union: Political Sources of an Economic Liability." *Journal of Economic Perspectives* 11, no. 4: 23–42.

——— (1997b): "EMU and International Conflict." *Foreign Affairs* 76, no. 6: 60–73.

Flowers, Edward B., and Francis A. Lees (2002): *The Euro, Capital Markets and Dollarization.* Lanham/Oxford: Rowman and Littlefield.

Fratianni, Michele, and Jürgen von Hagen (1992): *The European Monetary System and European Monetary Union.* Boulder, CO: Westview.

Frenkel, Jacob A., and Morris Goldstein (1993): "Monetary Policy in an Emerging European Economic and Monetary Union: Key Issues." In *International Finance: Contemporary Issues,* ed. Dilip K. Das, 187–97. London: Routledge.

——— (1998): "The Euro: Who Wins? Who Loses?" *Foreign Policy* 11, 25–40.

Frieden, Jeffry A. (1991): "Invested Interests: The Politics of National Economic Policies in a World of Global Finance." *International Organization* 45, no. 4: 425–451.

——— (2002): "Real Sources of European Currency Policy: Sectoral Interests and European Monetary Integration." *International Organization* 56, no. 4: 831–860.

Frieden, Jeffry A., Daniel Gros, and Erik Jones, ed. (1998): *The New Political Economy of EMU.* Boulder, CO: Rowman and Littlefield.

Garrett, Geoffrey (1994): "The Politics of Maastricht." In *The Political Economy of European Monetary Unification,* ed. Barry Eichengreen and Jeffry Frieden, 47–65. Boulder. CO: Westview.

——— (1998): *Partisan Politics in the Global Economy.* New York: Cambridge University Press.

Giavazzi, Francesco, and Alberto Giovannini (1989): *Limiting Exchange Rate Flexibility: The European Monetary System.* Cambridge, MA: MIT Press.

Giavazzi, Francesco, and Marco Pagano (1988): "The Advantages of Tying One's Hands: EMS Discipline and Central Bank Credibility." *European Economic Review* 32: 1055–1082.

Gilpin, Robert (1987): *The Political Economy of International Relations.* Princeton: Princeton University Press.

Giovannini, Alberto (1995): "Economic and Monetary Union: What Happened?" In *The Debate on Money in Europe,* ed. Alberto Giovannini. Cambridge: MIT Press.

Goddard, C. Roe (2003): "The International Monetary Fund." In *International Political Economy: State-Market Relations in the Changing Global Order,* ed. C. Roe Goddard, Patrick Cronin, and Kishore C. Dash, 241–267. Basingstoke, Hampshire: Palgrave Macmillan.

Goddard, C. Roe, Patrick Cronin, and Kishore C. Dash, ed. (2003): *International Political Economy: State-Market Relations in the Changing Global Order.* Basingstoke, Hampshire: Palgrave Macmillan.

Goodhart, Charles (1990): "Economists' Perspectives on the EMS: A Review Essay." *Journal of Monetary Economics,* 26, no. 3: 471–487.

Goodman, John B. (1992): *Monetary Sovereignty: The Politics of Central Banking in Western Europe.* Ithaca: Cornell University Press.

Grieco, Joseph M. (1995): "The Maastricht Treaty, Economic and Monetary Union, and the Neo-Realist Research Programme." *Review of International Studies* 21: 21–40.

Gros, Daniel, and Niels Thygesen (1998): *European Monetary Integration: From the European Monetary System to Economic and Monetary Union.* New York: Addison Wesley Longman.

Haan, Jakob de, and Silvester C.W. Eijffinger (2000): "The Democratic Accountability of the European Central Bank: A Comment on Two Fairy-Tales." *Journal of Common Market Studies* 38, no. 3: 393–407.

Hall, Peter A. and Robert J. Franzese, Jr. (1998): "Mixed Signals: Central Bank Independence, Coordinated Wage Bargaining, and European Monetary Union." *International Organization* 52, no. 3: 505–535.

Hallerberg, Mark (2003): Budgeting in Europe: Did the Domestic Budget Process Change after Maastricht? Paper presented at the 8th International Conference of the European Union Studies Association (EUSA), Nashville, Tennessee, March 27–29.

Hallet, Martin (2004): Fiscal Effects of EU Accession in Acceding Countries (mimeo).

Heipertz, Martin, and Amy Verdun (2004): "The Dog that Would Never Bite? On the Origins of the Stability and Growth Pact." *Journal of European Public Policy* 11, no. 5: 773–788.

Heisenberg, Dorothee (1999): *The Mark of the Bundesbank.* Boulder, CO: Lynne Rienner.

——— (2003): "Cutting the Bank Down to Size: Efficient and Legitimate Decision-Making in the European Central Bank After Enlargement." *Journal of Common Market Studies* 41, no. 3: 397–420.

Heisenberg, Dorothee, and Amy Richmond (2002): "Supranational Institution-Building in the European Union: A Comparison of the European Court of Justice and the European Central Bank." *Journal of European Public Policy* 9, no. 2: 201–218.

Henning, C. Randall (1994): *Currencies and Politics in the United States, Germany, and Japan.* Washington: Institute for International Economics.

——— (1996): "Europe's Monetary Union and the United States." *Foreign Policy* 102 (Spring): 83–100.

Henning, C. Randall and Pier Carlo Padoan (2000): *Transatlantic Perspectives on the Euro.* Pittsburgh, Pennsylvania: European Community Studies Association and Washington, D.C.: Brookings Institution Press.

Hodson, Dermot, and Imelda Maher (2002): "Economic and Monetary Union: Balancing Credibility and Legitimacy in an Asymmetric Policy Mix." *Journal of European Public Policy* 9, no. 3: 391–407.

Hosli, Madeleine O. (1998): "The EMU and International Monetary Relations: What to Expect for International Actors?" In *The European Union in the World Community* ed. Carolyn Rhodes, 165–191. Boulder, CO: Lynne Rienner.

Hosli, Madeleine (2000): "The Creation of the European Economic and Monetary Union: Intergovernmental Negotiations and Two-Level Games." *European Journal of Public Policy* 7 (2000): 744–766.

Hosli, Madeleine O., and Arild Saether, eds. (1997): *Free Trade Agreements and Customs Unions: Experiences, Challenges and Constraints.* Brussels/Maastricht: European Commission/European Institute of Public Administration.

Issing, Otmar (1999): "The Eurosystem: Transparent and Accountable or 'Willem in Euroland'." *Journal of Common Market Studies* 37, no. 3: 503–519.

Jones, Erik (2002): *The Politics of Economic and Monetary Union: Integration and Idiosyncrasy.* Lanham/Oxford: Rowman and Littlefield.

Kahler, Miles (1995): *Regional Futures and Transatlantic Economies.* Washington, DC: Brookings Institution Press.

Kalthenthaler, Karl C. (1998): *Germany and the Politics of Europe's Money.* Durham, NC: Duke University Press.

——— (2003): "Managing the Euro: European Central Bank Exchange Rate Policy Preferences." *European Union Politics* 4, no. 3: 329–349.

Kalthenthaler, Karl C., and Christopher J. Anderson (2001): "Europeans and Their Money: Explaining Public Support for the Common European Currency." *European Journal of Political Research* 40, no. 2: 139–170.

Kenen, Peter B. (1969): "The Theory of Optimum Currency Areas: An Eclectic View." In *Monetary Problems of the International Economy,* ed. Robert A. Mundell and Alexandre K. Swoboda. Chicago: University of Chicago Press.

——— (1992): *EMU after Maastricht.* Washington: Group of Thirty.

——— (1995): *Economic and Monetary Union in Europe: Moving Beyond Maastricht,* Princeton: Princeton University Press.

Kennedy, Ellen (1991): *The Bundesbank.* London: The Royal Institute of International Affairs.

Krugman, Paul (1991): *Currencies and Crises.* Cambridge, MA: MIT Press.

Kugler, Jacek, and John H.P. Williams (1994): "The Politics Surrounding the Creation of the EC Bank: The Last Stumbling Block to Integration." In *European Community Decision Making,* ed. Bruce Bueno de Mesquita and Frans N. Stokman, 185–228. New Haven: Yale University Press.

Leblond, Patrick (2003): Fiscal Convergence and Stability in the EMU: Alchemy, Missed Opportunities, and Commitment Institutions. Paper presented at the

Eighth Bienniel International Conference of the European Union Studies Association (EUSA), Nashville, Tennessee, March 27–29.

——— (2004): EMU Enlargement in a Post-World War II Perspective: The Role of Hegemony and Institutions. Paper presented at the annual meeting of the International Studies Association (ISA), Montreal, Canada, March 17–20.

Levitt, Malcolm, and Christopher Lord (2000): *The Political Economy of Monetary Union*. New York: St. Martin's.

Lijphart, Arend (1999): *Patterns of Democracy: Government Forms and Performance in Thirty-Six Countries*. New Haven: Yale University Press.

Loedel, Peter Henning (1999): *Deutsche Mark Politics: Germany in the European Monetary System*. Boulder, CO: Lynne Rienner.

——— (2002): "The European Central Bank: Exploring Institutional Independence and the Need for Reform." In *Institutional Challenges in the European Union*, ed. Madeleine O. Hosli, Ad M.A. van Deemen, and Mika Widgrén, 202–226. London/New York: Routledge.

Lohmann, Susanne (1998): "Federalism and Central Bank Independence: The Politics of German Monetary Policy, 1957–1992." *World Politics* 50: 401–446.

Ludlow, Peter (1982): *The Making of the European Monetary System: A Case Study of the Politics of the European Community*. London: Butterworth Scientific.

Martin, Lisa L. (1994): "International and Domestic Institutions in the EMU Process." In *The Political Economy of European Monetary Unification*, ed. Barry Eichengreen and Jeffry Frieden, 87–106. Boulder, CO: Westview Press.

McKinnon, Ronald I. (1963): "Optimal Currency Areas." *American Economic Review* 53, no. 4: 717–725.

——— (1993): "The Rules of the Game: International Money in Historical Perspective." *Journal of Economic Literature* 31: 1–44.

——— (2004): "Optimum Currency Areas and Key Currencies: Mundell I versus Mundell II." *Journal of Common Market Studies* 42, no. 4: 689–715.

McNamara, Kathleen R. (1998): *The Currency of Ideas*. Ithaca, NY: Cornell University Press.

——— (1999): "Consensus and Constraint: Ideas and Capital Mobility in European Monetary Integration." *Journal of Common Market Studies* 37, no. 3: 455–476.

Minford, Patrick (1993): "The Path to Monetary Union in Europe," *The World Economy* 16, no. 1: 17–27.

Moravcsik, Andrew (1998): *The Choice for Europe. Social Purpose and State Power from Messina to Maastricht*. Ithaca: Cornell University Press.

Mundell, Robert A. (1960): "The Monetary Dynamics of International Adjustment Under Fixed and Flexible Exchange Rates." *Quarterly Journal of Economics* 74: 227–257.

——— (1961): "A Theory of Optimum Currency Areas." *American Economic Review* 51, no. 4: 657–665.

——— (1962): The Appropriate Use of Monetary and Fiscal Policy for Internal and External Stability. IMF Staff Papers 9, no. 1: 70–79.

——— (1963): "Capital Mobility and Stabilization Policy under Fixed and Flexible Exchange Rates." *The Canadian Journal of Economics and Political Science* 29, no. 4: 475–485.

Neal, Larry, and Barbezat, Daniel (1998): *The Economics of the European Union and the Economies of Europe*. London: Oxford University Press.

Oatley, Thomas H. (1997): *Monetary Politics: Exchange Rate Cooperation in the European Union*. Ann Arbor: University of Michigan Press.

Padoa-Schioppa, Tomaso (1994): *The Road to Monetary Union in Europe: The Emperor, the Kings, and the Genies*. Oxford: Clarendon Press.

Peters, Patrick F.H.J. (1996): "The Development of the Euro as a Reserve Currency." *European Foreign Reserve Review* 2: 509–533.

Portes, Richard and Hélène Rey (1998): "The Emergence of the Euro as an International Currency." *Economic Policy* 26 (April): 305–332.

Qvigstad, Jan Fredrik (1992): *Economic and Monetary Union (EMU): A Survey of the EMU and Empirical Evidence on Convergence for the EC and the EFTA Countries*. Geneva: European Free Trade Association (EFTA).

Sandholtz, Wayne (1993): "Choosing Union: Monetary Politics and Maastricht." *International Organization* 47, no. 1: 1–39.

Simmons, Beth A. (1994): *Who Adjusts? Domestic Sources of Foreign Economic Policy During the Interwar Years, 1924–1939*. Princeton, N.J.: Princeton University Press.

Spero, Joan E., and Jeffrey A. Hart (2003): *The Politics of International Economic Relations*. Belmont, CA: Thomson/Wadsworth.

Stone Sweet, Alec, and Wayne Sandholtz, ed. (1998): *Supranational Governance: The Institutionalization of the European Union*. Oxford: Oxford University Press.

Story, Jonathan (1988): "The Launching of the EMS: An Analysis of Change in Foreign Economic Policy." *Political Studies* 36: 397–412.

Strange, Susan (1972): "The Dollar Crisis 1971." *International Affairs* 48: 191–215.

Tavlas, George S. (1993); "The Deutsche Mark as an International Currency." In *International Finance: Contemporary Issues,* ed. Dilip K. Das, 566–579. London: Routledge.

Tavlas, George S., and Yuzuru Ozeki (1992): The Internationalization of Currencies: An Appraisal of the Japanese Yen. Occasional Paper 90, Washington: International Monetary Fund.

Thomsen, Stephen, and Stephen Woolcock (1993): *Direct Investment and European Integration,* New York: Council on Foreign Relations Press.

Triffin, Robert (1960): *Gold and the Dollar Crisis: The Future of Convertibility*. New Haven: Yale University Press.

————— (1979): "The American Response to the European Monetary System." In *The European Monetary System: Its Promises and Prospects*, ed. Philip H. Trezise, 60–80. Washington: The Brookings Institution.

Tsoukalis, Loukas (1977): *The Politics and Economics of European Monetary Integration*. London: Allen and Unwin.

————— (1999): "Economic and Monetary Union: The Primacy of High Politics." In *Policy-Making in the European Union,* ed. Helen Wallace and William Wallace, 279–299. Oxford: Oxford University Press.

Verdun, Amy (1999a): "The Role of the Delors Committee in the Creation of EMU: An Epistemic Community?" *Journal of European Public Policy* 6, no. 2: 308–328.

———— (1999b): "The Institutional Design of the EMU: A Democratic Deficit?" *Journal of Public Policy* 18, no. 2: 107–132.

———— (2000): *European Responses to Globalization and Financial Market Integration. Perceptions of EMU in Britain, France and Germany.* Houndmills/Basingstoke: Palgrave MacMillan.

Verdun, Amy and Thomas Christiansen (2001): "The Legitimacy of the Euro: An Inverted Process?" *Current Politics and Economics of Europe* 10, no. 3: 265–288.

Verdun, Amy, ed. (2002): *The Euro: European Integration Theory and Economic and Monetary Union.* Lanham, Maryland: Rowman and Littlefield.

Viner, Jacob (1950): *The Customs Union Issue.* New York: Carnegie Endowment for International Peace.

Walsh, James I. (1994): "Politics and Exchange Rates: Britain, France, Italy, and the Negotiation of the European Monetary System." *Journal of Public Policy* 14, no. 3: 345–369.

———— (2000): *European Monetary Integration and Domestic Politics: Britain, France, and Italy.* Boulder, CO: Lynne Rienner.

Weinrichter, Norbert (2000): The World Monetary System and External Relations of the EMU: Fasten your Safety Belts! European Integration Online Papers (EioP), 4, 1. Available at http://eiop.or.at/eiop/texte/2000-010a.htm.

Weishaupt, J. Timo (2003): The Power of One: The Euro. Paper presented at the Eighth Biennial International Conference of the European Union Studies Association (EUSA), Nashville, Tennessee, March 27–29.

Wolf, Dieter, and Bernhard Zangl (1996): "The European Economic and Monetary Union: 'Two-level Games' and the Formation of International Institutions." *European Journal of International Relations* 2, no. 3: 355–393.

Woolley, John T. (1984): *Monetary Politics.* Cambridge: Cambridge University Press.

———— (1992): "Policy Credibility and European Monetary Institutions." In *Euro-Politics: Institutions and Policymaking in the 'New' European Community,* ed. Alberta Sbragia, 157–90. Washington: Brookings Institution.

Wyplosz, Charles (1997): "EMU: Why and How It Might Happen." *Journal of Economic Perspectives* 11, no. 4: 3–21.

Yarjani, Javad (2002): The Choice of Currency for the Denomination of the Oil Bill. Presentation April 14, Oviedo, Spain. Available at http://www.opec.org/NewsInfo/Speeches/sp2002/spAraqueSpainApr14.htm.

Index

About the Book

Tackling the alphabet soup of European Union treaties, structures, and policies, this straightforward introduction demystifies the European Economic and Monetary Union (EMU).

Hosli first traces the history of monetary integration in Western Europe and discusses the political and economic factors that led ultimately to the establishment of EMU and the euro. Then—in language accessible to the nonspecialist—she explains how it actually works. Ranging from institutions to performance to the impact of the euro both within Europe and on the international monetary system, she provides a welcome primer on this new phenomenon in the global political economy.

Madeleine O. Hosli is associate professor of international relations at Leiden University. She is coeditor of *Institutional Challenges in the European Union*.